I0887723

The National Holocaust Museum and the Hollandsche Schouwburg

Observe, reflect, act

Editors Annemiek Gringold & Asjer Waterman

Jewish Cultural Quarter | Waanders Publishers, Zwolle

Contents

Wallpaper of anti-Jewish measures

The regulations and auxiliary orders with which the Nazis carried out the persecution of the Jews of the Netherlands are listed on the walls of *The Netherlands and the Shoah* galleries. They describe the chronology of the Nazi persecution. The directives are reproduced on the cover, the endleaves and pages 1, 2, 87, 88, 159 and 160.

Foreword

Femke Halsema

mayor of Amsterdam

There can be only one response to the opening of the National Holocaust Museum: at last!

The background, realisation and need for the museum is the subject of this volume.

Three quarters of the Jewish population and almost all the Roma and Sinti in the Netherlands were murdered in the Second World War. Amsterdam, where Jews had enriched the city, building flourishing communities over hundreds of years, lost 61,000 of its 80,000 Jewish inhabitants amid the Third Reich's systematic, industrial-scale destruction.

How could it have happened? It's a question that keeps coming back whenever we're reminded of those cold statistics and the personal testimonies that accompany them. And it's a question that urges us on to study and spread the knowledge about what took place.

The murder of the Jews was the final act in a systematic process. Segregation, isolation, denial of rights through countless anti-Jewish regulations preceded the deportations and mass destruction.

In several Dutch cities, including Amsterdam, many fellow citizens came out in protest against these crimes, in particular in the strike of 25 February 1941. Many Jewish and non-Jewish heroes were active in the resistance and saved lives during the war.

Yet we know that others collaborated, betrayed and remained indifferent. In the Netherlands the government, including the municipality of Amsterdam, fell seriously short in its moral duty towards the city's Jewish citizens, before, during and after the Second World War.

There will be a time when no one remains to tell us firsthand about the persecution of the Jews. So it's all the more painful that antisemitism has raised its ugly head again in recent years. This is unacceptable. Happily, many are ready and willing to combat antisemitism, to continue studying the Holocaust and to gather new knowledge. For that, the National Holocaust Museum is essential.

The Holocaust is not only about what happened to the Jews all those years ago. It sets a moral standard for a society made up of minorities to be able to live together in peace. And that means never forgetting where those first steps to segregation can lead.

Abel Herzberg came from Amsterdam and survived Bergen-Belsen concentration camp. In a collection of essays in which he reflects on that period in the camp he wrote what might be a fitting motto for the museum and this book:

'If knowledge of these events can help us achieve an insight into what people are capable of, and what people may be made to do if they aren't careful, then much will have been gained.'

A National Holocaust Museum: Why?

Emile Schrijver

director Jewish Cultural Quarter

When Amsterdam's Jewish Cultural Quarter announced in 2015 that a National Holocaust Museum would be built on Plantage Middenlaan, one of the questions that I found particularly surprising was why it was still needed. The presentation at the Hollandsche Schouwburg had worn thin and still reflected views on the persecution of Dutch Jewry and the Holocaust of the 1990s. Moreover, the generation born during the war was now elderly and a time was approaching when there would be no one left to testify from personal experience. Furthermore, teachers at various levels were feeling increasingly uncomfortable about discussing the Holocaust, while rising antisemitism was causing considerable concern. And even so, that question was still being asked.

In the Netherlands, museums have tended to focus on particular, mainly local aspects of the murder of 102,000 Jews from the Netherlands. Naturally, the national dimension is also addressed at major historical locations such as Westerbork transit camp, Anne Frank House and Kamp Vught. Yet in all these places, this wider view of the destruction of Dutch Jewry is generally (although not only) employed to provide a context for the presentation of what happened there. Amsterdam Rijksmuseum's permanent presentation shows the eradication of the country's Jewish population as an aspect of Dutch history in a small display that reflects little of the complexity of the Shoah in the Netherlands. The National Holocaust Museum is the first to place the history of all the Jews in the Netherlands during the war at the heart of its permanent presentation. In so doing it pursues quite a different goal from that of other museums. Yet that history also has local, regional, national and international dimensions which are addressed wherever possible.

Another aspect of the National Holocaust Museum also goes some way to explaining why the museum is necessary. Anyone developing a museum such as this, almost eighty years after the end of the war, must be prepared to examine the impact of the Holocaust on the postwar world. The ease with which comparisons with the Holocaust have been employed in discussions of corona regulations or Middle-East wars clearly demonstrates that need. Yet it's not only about contemporary issues. Modern ideas about genocide, crimes against humanity, (transgenerational) trauma, human rights, the rule of law – the list goes on – are a direct consequence and at the very least cannot be viewed without reference to the effect of the Holocaust. In that sense, the National Holocaust Museum is first and foremost about all of us, society, humanity.

One of the most profound dilemmas a museum faces when dealing with violent atrocities concerns the detail with which these are presented and discussed. Each still or moving image requires an assessment: what is that exhibit showing, who created it, when and where and why. And in the case of living persons in the camps or the bodies of those murdered there, each time the same degree of awareness is needed to measure the desirability and impact of that particular image in a museum context, yet also, and above all, the integrity and the dignity of the victims shown. These are some of the hardest decisions when developing a museum like this. The need for historical accuracy in a time when the Holocaust is often downplayed and denied requires the images to be shown, and that makes these ethical considerations even more important.

This is different when it comes to text. The central assignment to the exhibition makers was to tell the history factually, unadorned. That may seem obvious, but it's far from that. While people may be increasingly reluctant to talk in explicit terms about the murder of six million Jews, it remains vital that we preserve the Holocaust as a moral touchstone, a unique historical event that demonstrates what may eventually happen if we allow one group to take away another's humanity, their property, their culture, segregate them and in the end systematically murder them. Clarity and transparency were the aim when editing these museum texts, as well as accessibility for the principal target group: those who come to learn. And that's not just schoolchildren. It includes students and a whole range of adults from all kinds of backgrounds.

The digital revolution has blessed us in many ways, yet undeniably it has placed the reliability of the information it supplies and the news it delivers under enormous pressure. Democratising access to information does not necessarily make it more trustworthy. The Holocaust, like antisemitism, is a subject on which a lot of dependable information can be found online, yet also a lot that is rather less dependable, potentially incorrect and disingenuous. The National Holocaust Museum provides an essential counterbalance and plays a key role in reaching out to a younger generation whose only source of information is often digital and yet through school will nevertheless visit our museum.

We have designed our educational programmes to provide that counterweight, for which it's also necessary to know and to address the assumptions that these young people bring to the museum. It's vital if we're to connect with them, especially those who come with alternative opinions. Only then are museum docents able to tackle, and where appropriate, correct inherent misconceptions or alternative perspectives. We have also kept this in mind when writing the texts accompanying the museum displays, while I ASK, the education method developed by the Jewish Cultural Quarter, is the foundation for all the texts and other products provided in the museum's education programmes and elsewhere.

It is also significant that we have developed the National Holocaust Museum as part of the Jewish Cultural Quarter. While other Holocaust museums struggle to define who their message actually represents and who has ownership of that message, this museum gives us all the space we need to present the history of the murder of the Netherlands' Jews in the Holocaust and at the same time to show the wealth of Jewish culture, history, religion and contemporary engagement at our other locations. That creates a new balance which enables us to present both sides of Jewish history, the beauty and the horror, to the full.

Museums are more than a permanent display these days, far more. Modern museums attempt increasingly to offer a complementary ensemble of activities. Permanent presentations and temporary shows, educational packages, additional and independent events and dedicated online content all come together to provide a comprehensive programme. This enables us to respond quickly and effectively to fast moving current issues, to respond to social pressures, while preserving sufficient space in house to examine the museum's content more profoundly through conversations with witnesses, conferences, receiving pupils, students and others engaged in learning, and through carefully redacted online content. It is that ensemble which will prove the impact of the National Holocaust Museum.

Sadly, antisemitism is once again asserting itself on the streets of the Netherlands. We are well aware how easy it is to ignite that dormant touchpaper and we recognise how insecure Jews still feel in Dutch society. The need for a National Holocaust Museum has not been questioned for some time. The new museum is not only there to address the often shocking lack of knowledge about the Holocaust; its comprehensive presentation is also there to show what happens when we allow society to segregate population groups. It highlights the consequences of not naming antisemitism and all forms of discrimination and exclusion, not fighting against them vigorously, and letting them persist without taking responsibility for the consequences of such attitudes. Those who visit the National

Holocaust Museum will never be able to say that they don't understand what it means to segregate people and dehumanise them. We consider it an honour and a moral duty to give the history of the Holocaust in the Netherlands a permanent place in our collective memory. In remembrance of all the victims and as a respectful celebration of each cruelly terminated life.

The Netherlands and the Shoah

The permanent exhibition

Annemiek Gringold

In the Shoah, the Nazis and their accomplices murdered around six million Jewish children and adults, more than 100,000 of whom from the Netherlands. Their history is one of segregation, confinement, deportation and murder, yet also of resistance and rescue.

◁ **A display of medals won by members of a Jewish gymnastics club in The Hague: Joodsche Gymnastiek-Vereeniging 's Gravenhage, 1937.** Jewish Museum collection.

The war that Nazi Germany unleashed in 1939 followed over six years of propaganda and oppression and was to last another six years. The vast majority of Germany's population endorsed their leader Adolf Hitler's policies and carried them out, as Nazi Germany occupied and annexed much of Europe with military force and strategy. Yet the Second World War and the destruction of European Jewry are actually two parallel histories. They happened at the same time, and they were connected and affected each other profoundly. The fighting provided cover for the persecution of Jews. The *Netherlands and the Shoah* presentation at the National Holocaust Museum shows how the Shoah unfolded in the Netherlands and what the Jews of the Netherlands experienced. Displays of objects, photos, films, texts, light and sound explain how the persecution of the Jews in the Netherlands happened. This article describes the history of the Shoah in the Netherlands as shown in the presentation. Elsewhere in this volume, the ideas behind the museum presentation and the design choices we made are discussed in greater detail.

Netherlands and the Shoah opens with an installation showing the two parallel histories. Twenty colour photos, still relatively rare in 1945, show the devastation in a score of cities and landscapes at the end of the war. Much of Europe lay in ruins, as did parts of Asia. In front of these, a huge black-and-white photo shows the devastation of human life: a young Jewish boy walking past rows of corpses in the newly liberated Bergen-Belsen. The boy is Sieg Maandag. He was from Amsterdam. His prewar life was forever lost and he would remain traumatised by what he had seen and experienced as a victim of Nazi persecution. He would live his life as a husband, father and artist, unable to ever distance himself from Bergen-Belsen. Like the others who survived the Shoah, he was left to pick up the pieces as best he could. It was the Shoah rather than the war that represents a fissure in modern history: the measure of ultimate evil on which the rules of today's international order and cooperation are founded.

Jewish life before the war

Having introduced the theme, the presentation brings visitors to the eve of the Shoah in the Netherlands. An impression of Jewish life before the war emphasises the diversity of the Jewish population in the Netherlands. There were around two hundred Jewish communities. Jews lived with, alongside and parallel to non-Jews in a country riven by social divisions. Society in the Netherlands had grown around religious and political groups and their organisations. Each group looked after its own. With a population of 140,000, Jews were too few to match the Protestant, Catholic or socialist infrastructures in size, yet Jews had their own schools and healthcare and their own clubs and societies. Jews had long enjoyed equal rights and opportunities to thrive and prosper. They worked in government, in politics, the army, science and the arts. Jewish businesses flourished, while thousands of Jews belonged to the working class. Among the latter, many found it hard to make ends meet. Although prejudice against Jews persisted in the Netherlands, this rarely led to violent confrontation.

Rosa Schlamowitz arrived in the Netherlands on a kindertransport organised by Truus Wijsmuller. Rosa was holding this locket.
Jewish Museum collection.

Rise of Nazi Germany

Unrest continued to plague Europe after the First World War (1914-1918). In Germany, the terms of the Versailles peace treaty were widely resented: swathes of territory had been conceded and massive reparations had been imposed. The Great Depression of 1929 hit Germany hard, providing fertile ground for the rapid growth of the National Socialist German Workers Party (NSDAP or Nazi party). In 1933, its leader Adolf Hitler became chancellor and the country descended into dictatorship. Using propaganda and terror, the Nazis strengthened their hold on the population. In 1936, the German army moved into the demilitarised Rhineland, breaking a key provision of the Versailles treaty. Hitler later admitted that it was his most vulnerable moment. But the international response was muted. In 1938 came Germany's union or Anschluss with Austria, while at an international summit in Munich, Hitler made sure that his annexation of Czechoslovakia's frontier province, Sudetenland, would meet no opposition. A few months later, Nazi Germany swallowed Bohemia and Moravia. Time and again, other governments chose to appease Hitler rather than stop him.

The Nazi regime imposed rigid censorship on German culture and used the education system to spread Nazi ideology. Political opponents and dissidents received harsh and violent treatment. A boycott of Jews was organised. Jews were attacked and persecuted. In the Netherlands, Dutch fascists formed a party in 1931: Nationaal-Socialistische Beweging (NSB). At first, its antisemitism was not pronounced. But that changed in 1938 as German Nazis gained influence.

Refugees

In the 1930s, around half of Germany's five hundred thousand Jews sought refuge abroad, along with many non-Jews. Some arrived in the Netherlands as early as 1933, where the first exiles were generally welcomed. Attitudes soon changed, however, and Dutch policy towards Jewish asylum seekers did not differ much from those of other countries. This was fed in part by a growing prejudice against Jews. In October 1938, Nazi Germany expelled seventeen thousand Jews with a Polish background. Poland refused to admit them and so they were left stranded in no-man's land. In protest, a Polish Jew, Herschel Grynszpan assassinated a German diplomat in Paris, Ernst vom Rath. The Nazis fanned the nation's outrage into a frenzy of state-organised violence on 9 November 1938 that lasted through to the following day and became known as Kristallnacht. Thirty thousand Jewish men were taken prisoner and held in concentration camps, hundreds of synagogues were set on fire and thousands of Jewish businesses were ransacked. The flow of Jewish refugees became a flood, to which the Netherlands responded by closing the frontier. Only those in immediate physical danger were admitted. Detention in a concentration camp was not sufficient reason. Meanwhile, the Dutch government tried to send as many refugees as possible to other countries. And at the same time, in Berlin and Vienna, Truus Wijsmuller was negotiating with the Nazis with the approval of the Dutch government. She managed to get permission to send a train with ten thousand Jewish children out of Germany and Austria. Over eight thousand went via the Netherlands to Britain, while the remaining two thousand found refuge in the Netherlands.

In 1939, the Dutch Jewish community funded the construction of a refugee camp at Westerbork in the province of Drenthe. An earlier location near Paleis 't Loo had met with royal opposition. On 28 August 1939, the growing threat of war prompted the Dutch to mobilise. However, the three hundred thousand strong army was ill-equipped for modern warfare, as indeed the government and the civil service.

Within days, on 1 September, Nazi Germany attacked Poland. After a tense wait, on 9 April 1940 the Nazis invaded Denmark and Norway; on 10 May 1940, the Netherlands, Belgium, Luxembourg and France. Three days later, the Dutch government and royal family fled to England. On 14 May, the Nazis bombed Rotterdam. The Dutch had held out with the loss of around two and a half thousand Dutch civilians and two thousand troops.

Occupation

On 15 May 1940, the Dutch army surrendered and the Nazis took control. A civil administration under Austrian lawyer Arthur Seyss-Inquart set about imposing Nazi rule. Parliament was dismissed and democratic institutions were abolished. The Dutch civil service continued to function, supervised by two thousand German administrative staff. Gradually, the Nazis brought the Dutch administration into line with Nazi Germany. To guard against an invasion from England, more troops were posted in the Netherlands.

Jews faced impossible dilemmas when the Nazis invaded: whether to wait and see, to flee, or even to commit suicide. The new Nazi regime issued a string of regulations. All kinds of orders and instructions created a judicial structure in which Jews were stripped of their rights. Those Nazi regulations are displayed on the gallery walls. They surround visitors, giving a sense of the confined environment in which Jews lived. Remarkably, in all the new rules that appeared in 1940 the word Jew is rarely mentioned, although the form in which employees were required to show their Aryan parentage (*Ariërverklaring*) was clearly designed to identify Jews. The Nazis defined who they considered Jewish based on ancestry. Based on this they segregated society. Most non-Jews in the Netherlands gradually adjusted to the new situation; little changed in their daily routine.

Teaspoons and porcelain from Bijenkorf department store in Rotterdam, melted in the firestorm following the bombing of the city on 14 May 1940. Rotterdam Museum collection.

Each Jew could buy four stars at most: they were 4 cents each and one textile coupon. Jewish Museum collection.

Increasing segregation

Having imposed their definition of who they considered Jewish, the Nazis proceeded to compile lists. This occurred in stages. Initially, Jews were required to register with their municipality, stating their Jewish parents and grandparents. Schools registered Jewish teachers, and then Jewish pupils. The Nazis then drew up their own lists, and in September 1941, they ordered the Jewish Council, which they had set up to manage the Jewish population, to do likewise. The Jewish Council card index was preserved and can be seen in the museum. Over 160,000 cards, each representing one person, chart the entire Jewish population. The Nazis then issued a slew of new orders. They separated Jews from non-Jews in every walk of life: in public, at work, at play, in shops, housing, transport and relationships. They restricted access to transport, they confiscated property. New regulations prevented Jews from earning a living, reducing many to poverty. Having made it impossible for Jews to find employment, the Nazis organised labour camps where they put the jobless to work. Jews were taken there *en masse* in Dutch trains manned by Dutch staff. Then the Nazis imposed the yellow star: all Jews were required to wear the symbol on their clothes. The stars were produced by De Nijverheid, a formerly Jewish-owned cloth mill in Enschede, confiscated and placed under non-Jewish administration. In the summer of 1942, the Jews of the Netherlands were isolated, without rights. They had no access to official channels or the courts: they were outlawed.

For day-to-day matters such as healthcare, travel, control over personal bank balances, education, culture, purchase of yellow stars and access to information Jews had only the Jewish Council, branches of which were located in around sixty municipalities. By late 1941,

Amsterdam's Jewish Council was the sole representative body for all the Jews in the Netherlands, ostensibly serving as a state within a state. Copies of the weekly *Joodsche Weekblad* in which the Jewish Council published the latest Nazi regulations are displayed in the museum.

After May 1940, membership of the Dutch Nazi party, NSB, shot up. Antisemitic NSB members terrorised Jewish neighbourhoods in Amsterdam. These provocations culminated in violent confrontations and in February 1941, NSB member Hendrik Koot was mortally wounded. The Nazis rounded up hundreds of Jewish men as a reprisal, and deported them to a concentration camp. The raid sparked a wave of indignation among the Amsterdam population, culminating in the February Strike.

Resistance to the anti-Jewish regulations spread as opposition to the various orders, the denial of rights and segregation increased. Wilhelmina Westerweel-Bosdriesz, a non-Jewish resister, described how that developed in 1983: 'It was extremely subtle, step by step. You have to refuse to take that first step.' She recalled how the latest regulation prohibiting Jews from entering parks convinced her to take that first step by refusing to enter the park herself. It was the first of many courage acts of resistance that saved many Jewish lives. Her refusal to accept the denial of rights to Jews is projected in the exhibition amid the photos, documents and films that illustrate the exclusion of Jews from society at large.

A final series of regulations followed, including a total ban on travel. Then in the summer of 1942, the Nazis were ready to begin deporting the Jews from the Netherlands. On 26 June 1942, the Nazis announced that Jews would be notified to report to be set to work.

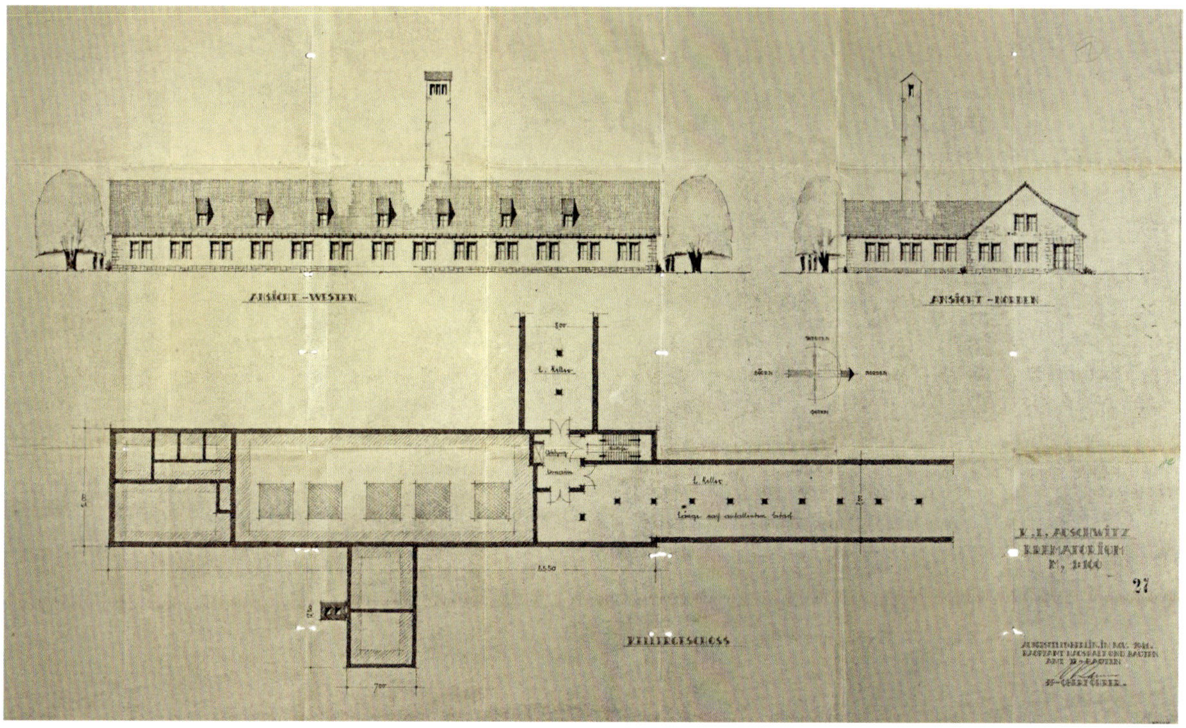

Blueprint of crematorium II at Auschwitz-Birkenau, November 1941. Yad Vashem collection.

A museum installation shows various kinds of perpetrators in day-to-day situations. Jewish Museum collection, photo by Thijs Wolzak.

Perpetrators

Individual perpetrators were involved at various levels in the persecution of Jews in the Netherlands. There were instigators, persecutors, collaborators, Jew hunters, camp guards, and murderers. Germans and Dutch. Some of them were ideologically motivated, others were loyal followers of the Führer, ambitious, opportunists or adventurers. They were all ordinary people: fathers, mothers, sisters, brothers. They lived in a world suffused in propaganda, fed on centuries of antisemitic prejudice. Blind to reason, they considered all Jews by definition a danger, subhuman, no longer recognising them as equals.

The murder starts

Throughout Europe, the Nazis stripped Jews of all rights, robbed them of their property and moved them into concentrated areas. In June 1941, Nazi Germany attacked the Soviet Union through eastern Poland. This brought many more Jews under Nazi control. Until then, the Nazis had considered expelling Europe's Jews, but now mass murder became a serious option. As the front shifted east, the Jews in the towns and villages were herded together and massacred. Hundreds of thousands were gunned down by mobile execution units, aided by local collaborators. Soon the Nazis devised new ways to kill more efficiently, hoping to spare the nerves of the perpetrators. They developed ways of killing huge numbers of people on an industrial scale in gas chambers.

The Nazis had used gas chambers before in a euthanasia programme. In 1939, they had set up six euthanasia centres where people they considered better off dead were treated accordingly. In January 1942, Nazis involved in the planning of the massacre of Jews met at Wannsee, in Berlin. There they decided to build extermination camps in Nazi-controlled Poland and devised plans to transport Jews from all parts of Europe to those camps.

The Nazi objective was to eradicate all of Europe's Jews. In Central and Eastern Europe, Jews had already been driven into ghettos and labour camps, making it easy for the Nazis to execute their plans. In the Netherlands, Jews were also ordered to move to Amsterdam or to specific parts of Amsterdam. Various deportation centres were set up, such as Hollandsche Schouwburg, from where Jews were sent to Westerbork transit camp and later also to camp Vught. Many Jewish men had already been detained and set to work in labour camps in the northeast of the country, leaving their families without any means of support. On 15 July 1942, the first train left Westerbork for the east and the mass murder of the Jews of the Netherlands began.

The Riessen family in Zeist made a hiding place in their home with blankets and this duvet. The Mazurs, a Jewish couple sheltering in their house, hid here whenever they were in danger of being discovered.
Jewish Museum collection.

The deportation of the first Jews from the Netherlands marked a new low for Europe. Heinrich Himmler, leader of the paramilitary Waffen-SS and German police, chose the arrival of that train at Auschwitz to inspect the extermination camp. He had approved the blueprints for the gas chambers and crematoria in November 1941. Now he came to see how they operated. He watched through a peephole in one of the hermetically sealed gas chambers as hundreds of women from the Netherlands were asphyxiated. He concluded his visit with an address to the women from that transport who had been selected for forced labour. Soon after the war Carla Lewenhoff-Kotowska remembered: 'Shortly after we arrived, a big roll-call was held where Himmler was also present. Himmler gave a speech in which he said that we Dutch women were far too 'ausgefressen' – overstuffed – that we would never be returning to Holland, but would perish in the mud. He took photos of us.'

Hidden from view

The mass murder of the Jews of the Netherlands happened far away, out of sight. Most Jews could only speculate about what deportation would mean. The Nazis employed an ominous term: 'set to work as family'. For many Jews it was reason enough to defy the threatened punishments and do their best to avoid deportation.

Around 28,000 Jews went into hiding in the Netherlands. They were taking a huge risk. Not least for the non-Jews who hid Jews. Betrayal and discovery were a constant danger. So the number of non-Jews prepared to risk helping Jews was relatively small. Various objects in the presentation illustrate the ways non-Jewish rescuers helped. When non-Jewish men were being conscripted to work in German factories in 1943, more hiding places were found. By then it was too late for most Jews. Only 16,000 of those in hiding survived the Shoah.

Many Jews looked for other ways to avoid deportation. Some tried to convince the Nazis that they were not really Jewish. Others hoped to escape because they had a non-Jewish partner or because their work gave them exemption. Finding a way abroad was expensive and there were no guarantees. Nevertheless, around six thousand Jews took that hazardous route. Various objects, including forgers' tools, a firearm and a cloak used to smuggle documents illustrate the part Jews played in the resistance in the Netherlands.

◁ **Camp garment from Auschwitz. The striped camp clothing dehumanised the prisoners further and took away their individuality.** NIOD collection, Beeldbank WO2.

Transit camp

For most Jews, escape or hiding were not an option. They were sent to Westerbork, a transit camp in Drenthe, and after January 1943 to a camp at Vught in North Brabant. Jews ended up in Nazi captivity in different ways. Some were ordered to report by post, others were detained in the street or at home. Jews were also arrested and rounded up in *razzias*, often in broad daylight. Dutch police helped carry out the deportations.

Some Jews left property with non-Jewish friends and neighbours prior to their deportation. Valuable items had already been forcibly confiscated. Once the owners had gone, Jewish homes were sealed and the remaining property removed for shipment to Germany. The Nazi regime obliterated some 350 years of Jewish history in the Netherlands.

Upon arrival in the transit camp Jews were registered and assigned to a barrack. There was one purpose behind Westerbork: to fill trains with people and send those trains to concentration- and extermination camps. Prisoners lived in trepidation from week to week. Camp jobs, connections and illness were all ways to avoid the next train. The Nazis used exemptions to manipulate their victims: a week's delay for one meant a place on the train for another. The camp was a transitory world, an ephemeral city on the heath. It had an infirmary, a school and a theatre. A make-believe world that gave a false sense of normality enabling the Nazis to organise the deportations with a minimum of fuss. Westerbork's commander even had a film made of that unreal world. At Vught, around twelve thousand Jews were imprisoned alongside political and other detainees. From there, deportees were often sent via Westerbork.

In 1944, the Nazi deportation of the country's Jews through Westerbork converged with the deportations of Roma and Sinti. As for the vast majority of Jews, the camp was their last known address in the Netherlands.

Murder

Over 107,000 Jews were deported from the Netherlands, many in freight wagons. The journey to the concentration and extermination camps in Germany and Nazi-occupied Czechoslovakia and Poland took two or three days. When they arrived, they faced the most extreme violence. Their last possessions were taken, and they were stripped of any remaining dignity.

The systematic, industrial-scale murder in the extermination camp was unprecedented. Jews were delivered into a system designed for mass murder. Most were gassed and cremated within hours, all trace of their existence destroyed. Others deemed useful were kept alive. Instead of a name, they were numbered. A further dehumanisation. Their number was tattooed on their arm. Most soon succumbed under a combination of hard labour, violence, starvation and exhaustion.

After the liberation

Three dates symbolise the end of the Shoah and the Second World War. On 27 January 1945, Auschwitz was liberated by the Soviet Red Army; on 8 May 1945, Nazi Germany surrendered, ending the Nazi slaughter in Europe. The Japanese surrender on 15 August 1945 marked the end of the Second World War.

Liberated Jews now faced the unimaginable loss of their family and loved ones. Government aid and the Dutch Red Cross were slow in coming, so many struggled to return and received an icy reception when they arrived.

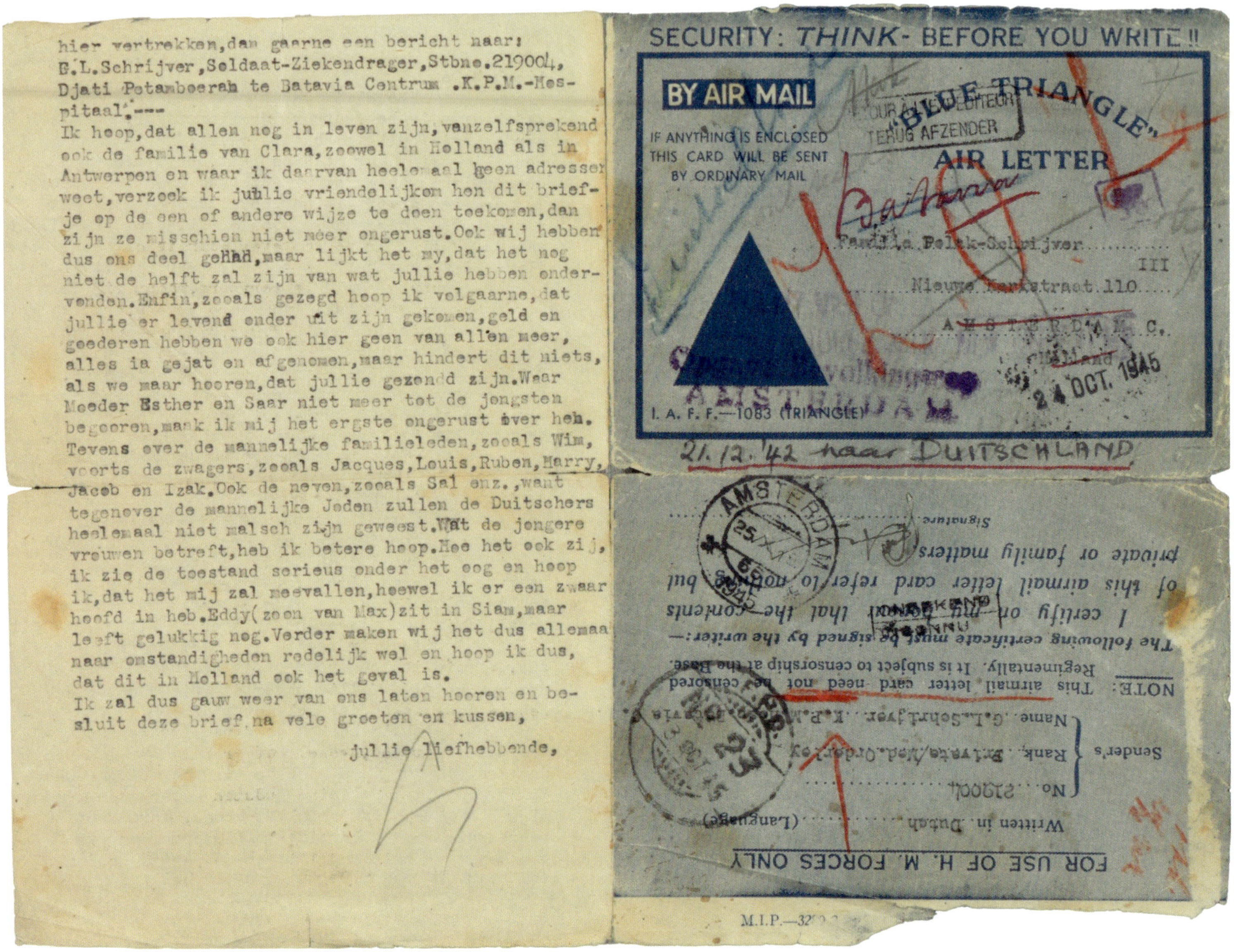

hier vertrekken,dan gaarne een bericht naar:
G.L.Schrijver,Soldaat-Ziekendrager,Stbne.219004,
Djati Petambeerah te Batavia Centrum .K.P.M.-Hos-
pitaal.---
Ik hoop,dat allen nog in leven zijn,vanzelfsprekend
ook de familie van Clara,zoowel in Holland als in
Antwerpen en waar ik daarvan heelemaal geen adressen
weet,verzoek ik jullie vriendelijken hen dit brief-
je op de een of andere wijze te doen toekomen,dan
zijn ze misschien niet meer ongerust.Ook wij hebben
dus ons deel gehad,maar lijkt het my,dat het nog
niet de helft zal zijn van wat jullie hebben onder-
vonden.Enfin,zooals gezegd hoop ik volgaarne,dat
jullie er levend onder uit zijn gekomen,geld en
goederen hebben we ook hier geen van allen meer,
alles is gejat en afgenomen,maar hindert dit niets,
als we maar hooren,dat jullie gezond zijn.Waar
Moeder Esther en Saar niet meer tot de jongsten
behooren,maak ik mij het ergste ongerust over hen.
Tevens over de mannelijke familieleden,zooals Wim,
voorts de zwagers,zooals Jacques,Louis,Ruben,Harry,
Jacob en Izak.Ook de neven,zooals Sal enz.,want
tegenover de mannelijke Joden zullen de Duitschers
heelemaal niet malsch zijn geweest.Wat de jongere
vrouwen betreft,heb ik betere hoop.Hoe het ook zij,
ik zie de toestand serieus onder het oog en hoop
ik,dat het mij zal meevallen,hoewel ik er een zwaar
hoofd in heb.Eddy(zoon van Max)zit in Siam,maar
leeft gelukkig nog.Verder maken wij het dus allemaal
naar omstandigheden redelijk wel en hoop ik dus,
dat dit in Holland ook het geval is.
Ik zal dus gauw weer van ons laten hooren en be-
sluit deze brief,na vele groeten en kussen,
jullie liefhebbende,

SECURITY: *THINK*- BEFORE YOU WRITE !!
BY AIR MAIL
IF ANYTHING IS ENCLOSED THIS CARD WILL BE SENT BY ORDINARY MAIL
"BLUE TRIANGLE"
AIR LETTER
TERUG AFZENDER
Familie Polak-Schrijver
III
Nieuwe Kerkstraat 110
AMSTERDAM C.
24 OCT. 1945
I. A. F. F.—1083 (TRIANGLE)
21.12.'42 naar DUITSCHLAND

After the Japanese defeat, Lou Schrijver, a Jew in the Dutch East Indies, wrote from Batavia to his relatives in the Netherlands. The letter came back undelivered and written on the envelop: 'To Germany, 1942'. Jewish Museum collection.

Persecution leaves a stigma. After the war survivors found themselves in a society which was even more antisemitic than before. Few people in the Netherlands wanted to hear their story, let alone acknowledge their suffering. For years, persecuted resisters were the only victims to receive compensation. The Dutch government made no distinction between Jews and non-Jews, only between Dutch and Germans. That resulted in some German Jews who had lived in the Netherlands before the war being held as potential enemies when they returned from the camps. Many Jews were unable to return home. Other people had moved in and their property had been taken. Information about missing relatives was also slow in coming. Many Jews still cherished the hope of seeing their loved ones again until well into the 1950s.

The experience of the decimated Jewish community in the postwar years reflects its gradual emergence from the shadow of war and a regained confidence. It was hard won. The struggle for the orphaned Jewish children, for inherited property and the reluctance to punish war criminals added to the pain of the survivors. Some felt that there was no future for the Jewish community in the Netherlands. A number moved to Israel. At first, Jews commemorated the Shoah within their own community.

Inscribed cardboard frame containing a portrait of an unidentified couple and possibly their son. Jewish Museum collection.

Gradually, however, the persecution of Jews received more recognition in national remembrance ceremonies. The wartime role of the Jewish Council remained a painful memory. There is still no consensus regarding the organisation's role. Survivors and their heirs are still campaigning and litigating regarding stolen property, restitution, property tax and duties, apologies and compensation. Postwar generations still bear the scars of the Shoah. And the Jewish community in the Netherlands is still vulnerable to increasing antisemitism.

As visitors leave *The Netherlands and the Shoah* exhibition three people, unidentified, meet their gaze. Perhaps they are a father, mother and son? All we know is that these people were deported. They wrote on their card: 'Don't forget us!'

Deprivation of rights and restitution

The legal system in the service of mass murder

Wouter Veraert

Deprivation of rights is a process of juridical exclusion. It involves the deliberate restriction of a person's ability to participate in society. That may be achieved by denying them their rights or by physical segregation. Those deprived of their rights find it harder to take part in public and economic activities. They become increasingly isolated and eventually bereft of all rights, outlawed.

'The first essential step on the road to total domination is to kill the juridical person in man.'
Hannah Arendt,
The Origins of Totalitarianism

◁ **Lagero shareholders register, Roosendaal, 1941. Each share belonging to the company's Jewish owners is transferred individually to the name of non-Jewish Rudolph Friedmann.** On loan Barenholz family.

The systematic deprivation of property rights and other rights of certain categories of people was a key aspect of Hitler's racist politics of persecution with which he aimed to create a totally Aryan society in both Germany and Nazi-held Europe. Those not considered by the Nazis to be Aryan, and by definition an enemy, had their rights curtailed. Jews were not the only people who forcibly lost their rights in German occupied Netherlands. Others also considered enemies of Nazi Germany, such as Roma and Sinti and Jehovah's Witnesses were persecuted and denied rights. This did not only affect individuals. The Nazis also took over organisations, such as Jewish businesses, Jewish and non-Jewish clubs and foundations, dismantling and liquidating them. In the summer of 1940, the German occupiers banned Freemasonry in the Netherlands, labelling the movement an enemy of national socialism. Masonic buildings, libraries, objects and property were brutally seized, sold and even destroyed across the country.

Measures against Jews

Anti-Jewish regulations were the main instrument used by the Nazis to implement their policy of juridical exclusion. In the Netherlands, they deprived Jews of their rights long before the first deportations from Westerbork in July 1942. This was reflected on the street by signs prohibiting Jews from entering, and the requirement to wear a yellow star. These physical images of legal exclusion have become familiar symbols of the persecution of the Jews. In fact, the Nazis used every means available to exclude Jews from many different fields of social and economic life, alternating tortuous juridical and bureaucratic regulations with terror on the street.

The German occupiers published their principal measures to deprive Jews of their rights in a periodical *Verordnungsblatt für die besetzten niederländischen Gebiete*. These introduced extreme legal injustice to the Netherlands. The infamous regulations are displayed on the walls of the National Holocaust Museum as a kind of wallpaper of crime. The Dutch-Jewish lawyer Abel J. Herzberg described the process of juridical exclusion and its oppressive impact in *Kroniek der Jodenvervolging* (Chronicle of the Persecution of the Jews). He explained the rationale behind the incremental deprivation of rights as follows: 'These were the methods, which created an ever-growing unrest, and increasingly accentuated that the Jew had ceased to be a legal subject, and was indeed bereft of all rights. In effect, outlawed, protected by no one, and – from the German perspective – not even susceptible to protection.'

Amsterdam notary A.A. Rambonnet used this stamp to notarise seized Jewish property. He had the dubious honour of having sold the most Jewish houses in a single day: 146 premises. Jewish Museum collection.

Another aspect of this process is material. For the Nazis, the deprivation of the rights of persecuted groups was a profitable business. They cynically used funds seized from victims to finance the deportations and to operate the concentration camps at Westerbork and Vught. As they systematically withdrew Jewish ownership rights to houses, agricultural land, household goods, shares, mortgages, leases, debts, insurance policies and other properties, these often came to be acquired by non-Jews. This led o a substantial shift in the distribution of property in Dutch society. The massive loss of property rights of Jews, Roma and Sinti as well as some other groups was not a matter between the victims and the Nazi regime alone. Many non-Jews and non-Jewish organisations in the Netherlands played an active part. Stockbrokers, notaries, bankers and insurers were among those closely involved in the process, often voluntarily ('if not, others will do it'), sometimes proactively soliciting orders. Some resisted, and here and there were protests. But without the active aid and participation of Dutch people and organisations not subject to persecution, the deprivation of rights during the war would not have been as extensive or intense. It was not until the end of the twentieth century that the Dutch state, financial institutions and various professional organisations apologised to the Jewish community for their conduct during the war and their unwillingness after the war to repair as far as possible the wrongs committed.

Safekeeping

As we have seen, little active resistance or protest was made against the systematic deprivation of rights: only a few individuals refused on principle to become involved. Many Dutch citizens and organisations that were not persecuted benefited by moving into houses that Jews had been forced to vacate, buying shares and other certificates that Jews had been required to submit to Lippmann, Rosenthal & Co. (LiRo, a bank run by the Nazis to acquire Jewish assets) on Sarphatistraat, by buying art that had belonged to Jews, or taking over their job, trade or company. Even more shocking are the cases in which Jews felt constrained to ask non-Jews to look after their valuables and possessions, whether for payment or not, and then returning after the war to find their safekeepers unwilling to return the property to the rightful owners or heirs. Many incidents like that occurred. Marga Minco described the situation eloquently in a short story: *Het Adres* (The Address). In *U wordt door niemand verwacht* (No one is expecting you), Michal Citroen cites examples of the chilly reception received by Jews returning to the Netherlands from the camps and from hiding. Like the story of Rita Boas's daughter, who knew shortly after the war who her mother had asked to look after her two Jugendstil vases: 'He's still alive. I saw him cycling in Amsterdam recently.

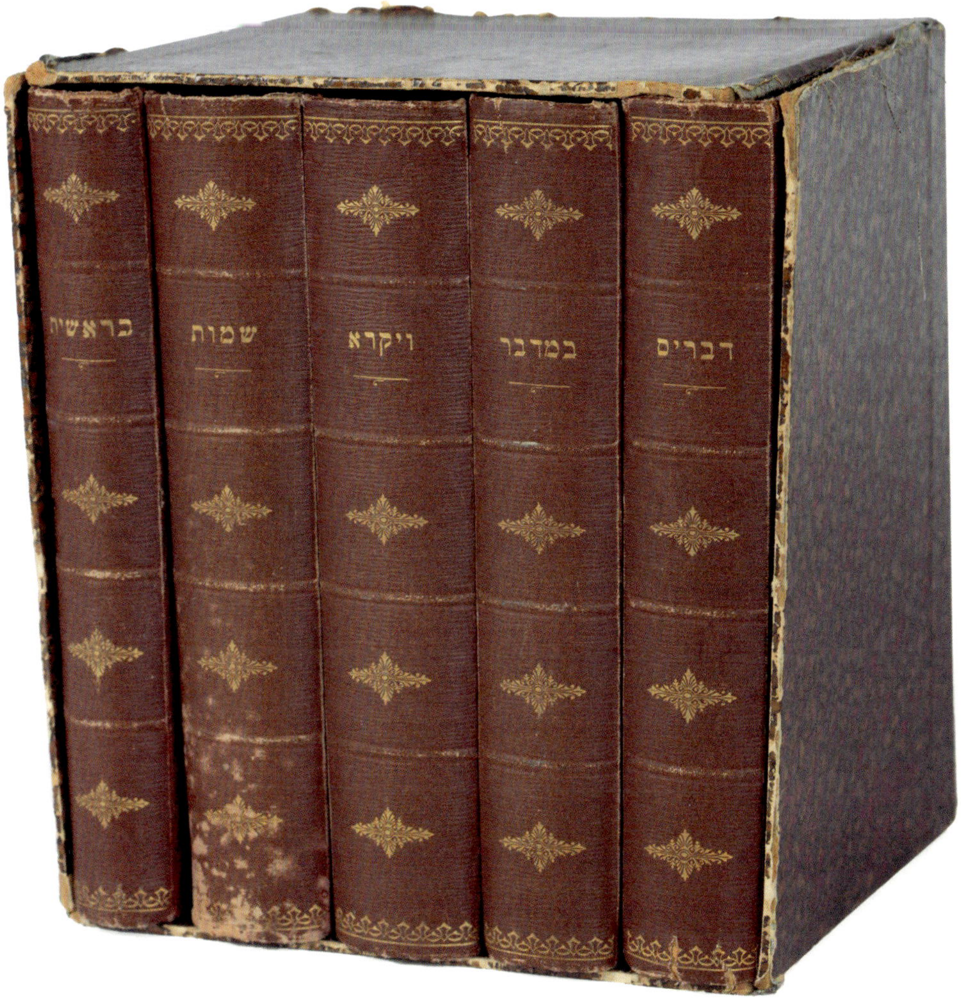

Gerard Sanders left this Chumash with non-Jews he knew and trusted shortly before going into hiding. They preserved the five-volume set, but Sanders himself was betrayed and murdered. They returned the Chumash to Sanders's heirs, who gave it to the museum. Jewish Museum collection.

I was about to call out: "Hey, where are my mother's vases?" but he looked petrified when he saw me and I thought: let it go.'

The machinery of juridical exclusion in the Netherlands was so extensive that many became involved by accident, for example on Amsterdam's stock market where shares change hands extremely fast. Not everyone who bought an item during the war was aware of its provenance. The involvement of so many participants and the huge sums and amounts of looted Jewish property concerned made postwar restitution in the Netherlands extremely complicated.

Alternative definition of administration

The measures displayed on the museum walls are just the tip of the bureaucratic iceberg: they provided a framework which each relevant body, Dutch included, would need to interpret and apply to specific cases. Leaving aside the organisational complexity, the basic plan for the seizure of property rights may be summarised as: registration, administration, sale – profits from the latter going exclusively to German organisations, not the rightful owners. The measures ordered that all Jewish-held property and rights be identified and registered. Thereafter, these would be placed under administration of *Verwalter* or *Treuhänder* as determined by one of several German bodies. Jewish firms would be placed under the *Verwaltung* of a Dutch or German Aryan *Treuhänder* appointed by the *Generalkommissar für Finanz und Wirtschaft*, while *Niederländische Grundstücksverwaltung* would appoint *Verwalter* to manage Jewish real estate. The infamous LiRo measures of 8 August 1941 and 21 May 1942 required all kinds of financial assets to be submitted to the already mentioned German institution which operated under the name of an established Jewish bank Lippmann, Rosenthal & Co. on Sarphatistraat, to foster confidence. LiRo became also responsible for the administration of these assets.

Administration is not really an adequate term. Under normal circumstances, a body entrusted with managing assets is responsible to the owner and may not dispose of them without the owner's permission. Here however, the legal notion of administration was turned upside down and used to divest Jews of all rights to make decisions about their assets. This was done quite simply: the measures stated that Aryan administrators were required only to follow the instructions of the German occupation authorities. Plus they were enabled to sell the assets they administered without the owner's permission.

An example is a regulation entitled 'Verordening van den Rijkscommissaris voor het bezette Nederlandsche gebied betreffende het joodsche grondbezit' (Measure by the Reich Commissioner for the occupied Netherlands regarding Jewish property) issued on 11 August 1941. It laid out clearly how to organise the registration, administration and sale (referred to as alienation) of Jewish assets without the owner's permission. Article 7 of this regulation stated that the administration of registered Jewish real estate was the responsibility of *Niederländische Grundstücksverwaltung* or an administrator appointed by this organisation. Article 8 stipulated that this body 'having taken over the administration' was authorised 'to perform [...] all legal transactions [...] pertaining to the proper administration of the Jewish property'; decisions by the Jewish rights holder were henceforth void. In a detailed pro-German commentary on this directive, Amsterdam lawyer M.M.G.Th. de Kort left no room for doubt about what the administration of Jewish property meant: 'Who does the administrator represent? The owner? That can hardly be the case, since appointments and dismissals are arranged without reference to the owner, and because the administrator was doubtless given that authority (including power of alienation) under article 8 against the owner's wishes.'

So who did the administrator represent? Here again the author of the commentary left little room for doubt: the Nazified Dutch state. 'To some extent, the administrator is the executor of the state, as stipulated in the directive. This relation is expressed in the duty of accountability to the state as discussed below.'

Legal foundation proves superfluous

The final step in the process of deprivation of property rights was sale by confiscators such as LiRo or individual Aryan administrators. But this was against a core principle of Dutch civil law which states that no one may dispose of another's property without permission. Yet the German occupier did not always expressly permit this practice in its directives. For example, in February 1942, LiRo began selling shares in large amounts on Amsterdam's stock market without the permission of the Jewish owners. They had been required to deposit their shares under the first LiRo measure, 'Verordening betreffende de behandeling van het joodsche geldelijke vermogen' (Measure regarding the management of Jewish financial assets) of 8 August 1941. LiRo sent the Jewish owners specified notifications of these unauthorised sales with a stamped message: 'This sale is in accordance with instructions received from the competent authority.' On the standard form, the preprinted text stating 'In accordance with your instructions we have sold for you' was struck out with a typewriter. However, the first LiRo measure made no reference to this revision. That drew protests. One of the more interesting objections is found in the archive of the Vereniging voor de Effectenhandel (Amsterdam Stock Exchange Association): copies of correspondence between an honest custodian of Jewish property and LiRo. LiRo had sold shares from the owner's portfolio at the Amsterdam Stock Exchange in early 1942 and had notified the administrator as usual. The latter protested, informing LiRo that he did not recognise LiRo's sale as a legal transaction. In a letter dated 9 April 1942, LiRo replied that it had no choice since 'the instructions we received are such that their legality is not a matter for discussion.' The administrator was not impressed and sent a new series of letters in protest. What makes this protest remarkable, and it was not the only one, is the way this administrator was able to embarrass LiRo with his technical legal argument regarding the legality of a sale without permission. In a second reply, LiRo had little else to say than to threaten the administrator and in an awkward aside to reveal that behind the 'competent authority' there lay a 'German organisation!' Once again, the administrator refused to be intimidated. He maintained his position that he as administrator would be failing his duty – and might be held accountable by the owner – if he were to sanction the illegal LiRo sale. And there the correspondence ends.

It was not just LiRo that struggled to present a cogent argument for the legality of the sales. The Dutch board of the Amsterdam Stock Exchange Association, under whose authority LiRo sales had been traded at the exchange, had no answer to the demands of Jewish owners who questioned the validity of the transactions. The board, with Amsterdam stockbroker Carel Overhoff in the chair, who was, as a result of German innovations in the structure of enterprises, the now mandatory 'strong leader', found itself in a difficult position. It had admitted LiRo to trade on the exchange floor by a controversial decision in September 1941. A month before, in August, together with the Amsterdamse Bankiersvereniging (Amsterdam Banking association), it had successfully lobbied the German authorities for a part in the sale of shares submitted to LiRo.

The board left the letters from anxious Jewish owners unanswered. At the same time, it asked Dr Albert Bühler who the 'competent authority' was that LiRo kept referring to when selling Jewish shares, and what the legal basis was for that authority. Bühler was the German *Beaufragte* at De Nederlandsche Bank (the Dutch central bank) and, in that capacity, a leading organiser of the sale of Jewish assets during the war. He replied that the sales had been ordered by Dr Hans Fischböck, *Generalkommissar für Finanz und Wirtschaft* in occupied Netherlands. Fischböck's order was *suprema lex* (the highest law), wrote Bühler, and LiRo had therefore been licensed to sell. The board accepted the explanation. Henceforth, Jewish owners would be informed by the Amsterdam Stock Ecxchange that LiRo sales could not be questioned since they were authorised by an unpublished instruction by a German authority that was apparently *suprema lex*.

Law in the service of power, power unconstrained by law

This episode shows that despite the intricate legal reasoning of the *Reichskomissar*'s directives, the German occupiers struggled to present the systematic deprivation of rights of Jews as lawful. In fact, there's a simple reason for the occupier's failure to provide a solid legal foundation for the sale of shares without permission of the owners. The main goal of the first LiRo measure was to encourage Jewish owners to surrender all their monetary assets quickly and without fuss: shares, cash, cheques, bank certificates, deposits et cetera. That would have gone a lot less smoothly if the first order had stated in as many words that those assets would be sold without their owners' permission, and the profits would be withheld. The measure was deliberately framed to give the impression that the regulation was intended purely to administer the assets for and on behalf of their owners.

The episode also illustrates how the Nazis used law as an instrument of power. In the totalitarian Nazi state, law was what government institutions interpreted as the will of the Führer, Adolf Hitler. In effect, the rule of law had already come to an end in the Netherlands when the Germans invaded. Henceforth, law was in the service of power, and power was no longer constrained by law. It would be incorrect to conclude from the remarkable precision of the anti-Jewish regulations and all the executive orders based on these that the deprivation of rights of the Jewish community and other groups came to fruition based purely on this body of occupation law. Because even those regulations could be brushed aside, to make way for secret directives or brute force if that were needed to achieve the political objectives. The anti-Jewish measures displayed on the museum walls in which legalised injustice is declared in all its shocking intricate, bureaucratic detail tell us only part of the story.

Extreme injustice in legal form

What remains unresolved is the extent to which the anti-Jewish regulations can be considered law. Their extreme injustice – denying equality before the law and other human rights, constitutional rights and basic principles of Dutch civil law – raises a difficult question: is this even law? Even if laws like this can indeed exist – which is the generally accepted opinion – these regulations contravened the regulations concerning the Laws and Customs of War on Land of the Hague Convention of 1907, to which Germany had also been a signatory. For that reason, it has often been lamented that in its judgment on judicial review of 12 January 1942, the Dutch Supreme Court (Hoge Raad) argued that Dutch courts lacked competence to review the content of all German measures for compliance with the Hague Convention, thereby recognising those measures as legally valid. Critics have stated that for citizens and companies still wondering whether to collaborate with the German occupiers, the Supreme Court's judgment helped to give the measures, including those shown on the museum walls, a sense of legitimacy.

In any case, the validity of the German anti-Jewish regulations was retroactively nullified on 17 September 1944. That day, the Dutch government in exile issued a Decree on Occupation Measures (Besluit bezettingsmaatregelen), known as E 93, the reference number of the official gazette (*Staatsblad*) in which the legislation was published. The Nazis most flagrant wartime measures appeared in E 93 under List A. These were the regulations which would be considered never to have had any validity, including all the regulations against Jews. List B contained the regulations which would cease to apply as soon as the Nazis had been expelled from the Netherlands. Finally, List C contained German regulations which would temporarily remain in force.

Museum visitors are surrounded by the texts of regulations, notifications and instructions that robbed Jews in the Netherlands of their rights. The regulations were assembled in annual volumes. Jewish Museum collection, photo byThijs Wolzak.

The painstaking struggle for restitution

The retroactive nullification by the Dutch government in London of the anti-Jewish measures in September 1944 had more than symbolic value. Invalidating these regulations enabled Jews to take part in judicial processes as equal citizens again. They were once more able to exercise their rights and to demand those rights in court, which they had been almost totally denied during the war. It was the first step towards restoration of rights, a long, hard struggle that the Jewish community and its representatives would wage in the period after 1945.

In the Netherlands, restoration of rights was based on an international Joint Declaration issued on 5 January 1943, a solemn statement made in London by eighteen allied governments, including the Netherlands. It stated that they would do everything in their power to end the widescale plunder by the Nazi aggressors and their accomplices. And they reserved the right to nullify any transactions linked to that plunder, however legal in form or appearance, and to reverse these. That international foundation for postwar restitution had a huge impact, and continues to affect matters relating to restitution after historical injustices beyond the Second World War and including the colonial past.

Lawyer Heiman Sanders helped many Jews seeking legal restitution in the postwar period. He received this dish in recognition for his work. Jewish Museum collection.

The path to restitution was laid out in the Netherlands in Besluit Herstel Rechtsverkeer (Decree on Restoration of Legal Relations), E 100, which the Dutch government issued along with E 93 on 17 September 1944. The form and content of the restitution process envisioned in London was notable for its extremely pragmatic approach and its occasionally relaxed handling of constitutional principles. For example, various executive bodies were given jurisdictional functions, while one particular body, Afdeling Effectenregistratie (Securities Division), even included representatives of the financial world who were involved in some of the cases they were hearing. The extraordinary design of the restitution process gave the finance minister, Pieter Lieftinck, enormous influence on its implementation. Fortunately, there was a jurisdictional body, Afdeling Rechtspraak (Judicial Division), that operated independently and impartially.

For groups that had been systematically deprived of their rights, restitution was important in other ways too. It was what would enable them to participate, once again, as equal citizens in legal and social-economic life. The restoration of their rights was going to ensure they had that opportunity. Yet that hope would be sorely tested. The restitution process was one among many policy objectives the country had set itself in the postwar reconstruction programme. Lieftinck strongly defended the interests of the Dutch treasury and other financial institutions considered essential to the economic reconstruction of the Netherlands. Those economic interests were constantly confounding the basic principle of restitution. According to that principle, those who had knowingly traded or acquired looted property could be ordered by the courts to restore those items to their original owner, or compensate the damage incurred. In May 1952, the Amsterdam Stock Exchange actually went on strike following a ruling by the Judicial Division that all banks and stockbrokers that had bought shares directly from LiRo were held liable and should pay compensation to the original Jewish owners.

This clash of interests plunged legal restitution in the Netherlands into a huge, unequal struggle in which the unexpectedly positive results that were achieved in the early 1950s were largely due to the success of one pugnacious individual, a Jewish lawyer named Heiman Sanders who, as the driving force behind the Commissie tot Bescherming der Aanspraken van Gedepossedeerden (Committee to Protect the Claims of the Dispossessed) managed to win a series of crucial court cases against the Dutch state, insurers, banks and stockbrokers between 1946 and 1952. In recognition for one of his greatest achievements – a case he helped win against the Dutch state involving the LiRo estate which was worth millions of guilders, resulting in substantially larger payments to Jewish creditors than had previously been anticipated – on 6 July 1952, the committee chair, noted jurist Eduard Meijers presented Sanders with an inscribed silver dish on behalf of all those concerned.

The unexpected success of Sanders and his fellow combatants did not close the book on restitution. There had been too many gaps and glitches in the 1940s and 50s for that. In the 1990s, restitution was once again high on the list of national and international priorities. Now it was unfinished business: the dormant Swiss bank accounts of Jews who had been murdered, the looted artworks that had not been returned to their rightful owners after the war and the failed procedures which had greatly increased the suffering of Jews returning from the camps and from hiding.

In the Netherlands, the discovery of the LiRo archive by *De Groene Amsterdammer* journalists in a building on Amsterdam's Herengracht refocused attention on the issue. Five research committees were appointed and Jewish organisations began negotiating with insurers, banks, the Amsterdam Stock Exchange and the Dutch government for recognition, an apology and restitution. A series of agreements followed in 1999 and 2000, in which both the Dutch government and insurers, banks and stock exchange apologised and paid financial compensation. Those sums were distributed in the form of Maror pensions to individual members of the Jewish community. Maror is an acronym for

In 1946, Mourits Vis of Bussum, who had survived the war in hiding, received a writ in the name of the Queen. He still owed taxes for the year 1942. Jewish Museum collection.

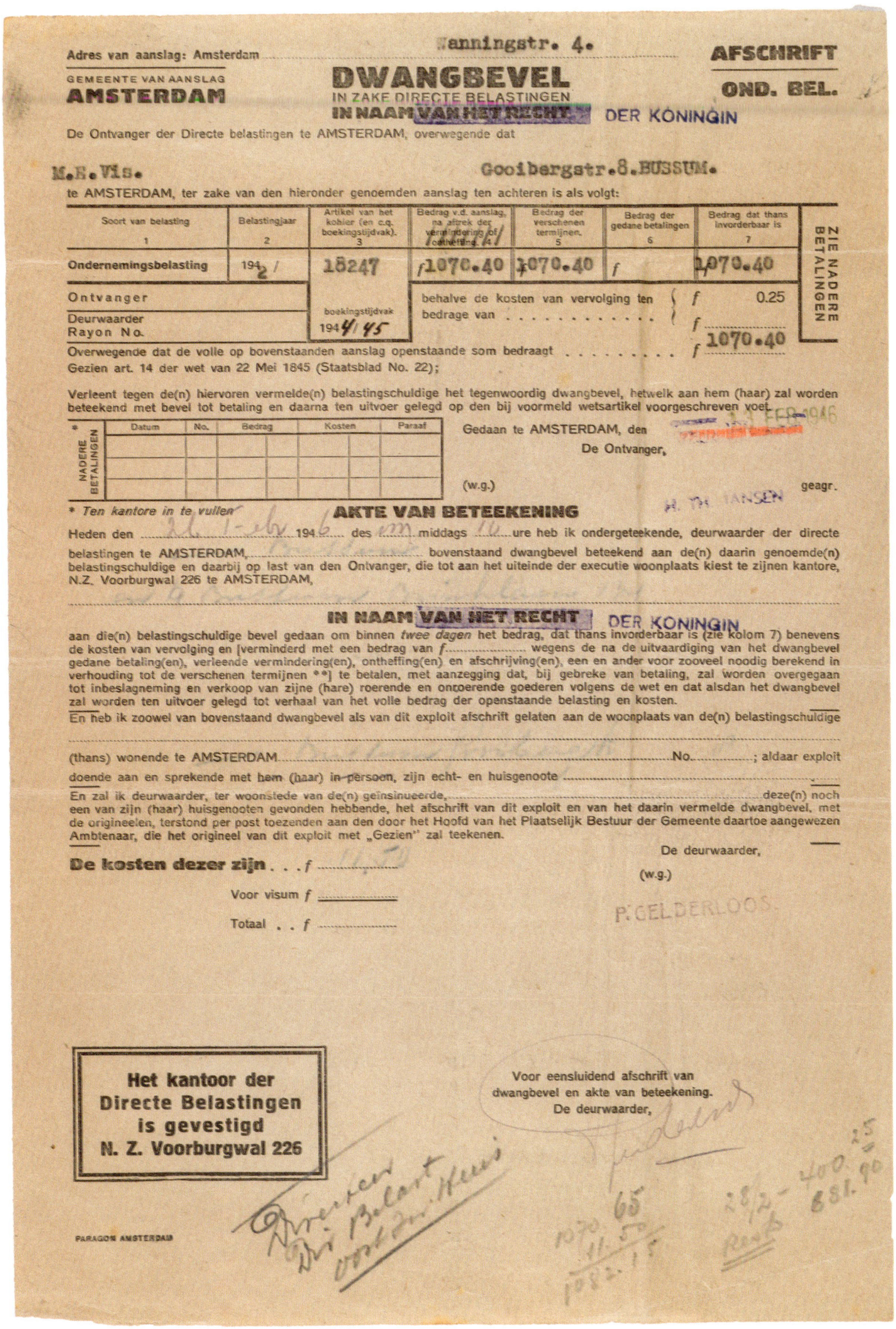

Adres van aanslag: Amsterdam ...... Wanningstr. 4.

AFSCHRIFT

OND. BEL.

GEMEENTE VAN AANSLAG
AMSTERDAM

DWANGBEVEL

IN ZAKE DIRECTE BELASTINGEN
IN NAAM ~~VAN HET RECHT~~ DER KONINGIN

De Ontvanger der Directe belastingen te AMSTERDAM, overwegende dat

M.E.Vis. Gooibergstr.8.BUSSUM.

te AMSTERDAM, ter zake van den hieronder genoemden aanslag ten achteren is als volgt:

Soort van belasting 1	Belastingjaar 2	Artikel van het kohier (en c.q. boekingstijdvak). 3	Bedrag v.d. aanslag, na aftrek der vermindering of ontheffing. 4	Bedrag der verschenen termijnen. 5	Bedrag der gedane betalingen 6	Bedrag dat thans invorderbaar is 7
Ondernemingsbelasting	1942 /	18247	f 1070.40	f 1070.40	f	f 1070.40

ZIE NADERE BETALINGEN

Ontvanger

Deurwaarder
Rayon No.

boekingstijdvak 1944/45

behalve de kosten van vervolging ten bedrage van .... f 0.25 f ......

Overwegende dat de volle op bovenstaanden aanslag openstaande som bedraagt .... f 1070.40

Gezien art. 14 der wet van 22 Mei 1845 (Staatsblad No. 22);

Verleent tegen de(n) hiervoren vermelde(n) belastingschuldige het tegenwoordig dwangbevel, hetwelk aan hem (haar) zal worden beteekend met bevel tot betaling en daarna ten uitvoer gelegd op den bij voormeld wetsartikel voorgeschreven voet.

* NADERE BETALINGEN	Datum	No.	Bedrag	Kosten	Paraaf

* Ten kantore in te vullen

Gedaan te AMSTERDAM, den 1? FEB 1946

De Ontvanger,

(w.g.) H. TH. JANSEN geagr.

AKTE VAN BETEEKENING

Heden den 26 Febr 1946 des nam middags ... ure heb ik ondergeteekende, deurwaarder der directe belastingen te AMSTERDAM, ... bovenstaand dwangbevel beteekend aan de(n) daarin genoemde(n) belastingschuldige en daarbij op last van den Ontvanger, die tot aan het uiteinde der executie woonplaats kiest te zijnen kantore, N.Z. Voorburgwal 226 te AMSTERDAM,

IN NAAM ~~VAN HET RECHT~~ DER KONINGIN

aan die(n) belastingschuldige bevel gedaan om binnen *twee dagen* het bedrag, dat thans invorderbaar is (zie kolom 7) benevens de kosten van vervolging en [verminderd met een bedrag van f .... wegens de na de uitvaardiging van het dwangbevel gedane betaling(en), verleende vermindering(en), ontheffing(en) en afschrijving(en), een en ander voor zooveel noodig berekend in verhouding tot de verschenen termijnen **] te betalen, met aanzegging dat, bij gebreke van betaling, zal worden overgegaan tot inbeslagneming en verkoop van zijne (hare) roerende en onroerende goederen volgens de wet en dat alsdan het dwangbevel zal worden ten uitvoer gelegd tot verhaal van het volle bedrag der openstaande belasting en kosten.

En heb ik zoowel van bovenstaand dwangbevel als van dit exploit afschrift gelaten aan de woonplaats van de(n) belastingschuldige

(thans) wonende te AMSTERDAM ...... No. ......; aldaar exploit doende aan en sprekende met ~~hem~~ (haar) ~~in persoon~~, zijn echt- en huisgenoote ......

En zal ik deurwaarder, ter woonstede van de(n) geïnsinueerde, ... deze(n) noch een van zijn (haar) huisgenooten gevonden hebbende, het afschrift van dit exploit en van het daarin vermelde dwangbevel, met de origineelen, terstond per post toezenden aan den door het Hoofd van het Plaatselijk Bestuur der Gemeente daartoe aangewezen Ambtenaar, die het origineel van dit exploit met „Gezien" zal teekenen.

De deurwaarder,

(w.g.) P. GELDERLOOS.

De kosten dezer zijn . . . f 11.50

Voor visum f ......

Totaal . . f ......

Het kantoor der Directe Belastingen is gevestigd N. Z. Voorburgwal 226

Voor eensluidend afschrift van dwangbevel en akte van beteekening.
De deurwaarder,

PARAGON AMSTERDAM

Morele Aansprakelijkheid Roof en Rechtsherstel (Moral accountability for looting and legal restitution), but it also means bitter in Hebrew: the bitter herb of the Pesach seder symbolising bitter times. A portion of the money was set aside for collective activities and good causes in the Jewish community. In the field of looted art and cultural objects, the Restitutions Committee is still active, advising on applications for the return of artworks unwillingly divested during the war. On a local level, researchers continue to study various aspects of postwar legal restitution relating to ground rent, real estate and companies.

After apologising in 2000 for the failures related to the postwar restitution process in the 1940s and 1950s, twenty years later the Dutch government apologised for the first time for the actions and failure to act of Dutch civil servants during the Second World War. On 26 January 2020, Dutch prime minister Mark Rutte declared at the national Holocaust remembrance ceremony in Amsterdam: 'When a group of fellow citizens were segregated, excluded and dehumanised by a murderous regime, we fell short. When authority represented a threat, our government institutions, the guardians of law and security, fell short.' That message was repeated a few months later by King Willem-Alexander in a speech delivered on National Remembrance Day, 4 May, precisely seventy-five years after the liberation of the Netherlands.

Fresh light on a fraught history

Architecture, stratification and articulacy

Esther Göbel

Together with the Hollandsche Schouwburg, the National Holocaust Museum in the former teacher-training college Hervormde Kweekschool and the adjacent new building represents a broad spectrum of the history of the Shoah: a history of segregation, persecution and murder, yet also a history of rescue, survival and solidarity.

◁ **The Hollandsche Schouwburg exterior with the five statues, 1917.** National Archive/Spaarnestad Photo/*Het Leven*, unidentified photographer.

Plantage before the war

The original Kweekschool and Hollandsche Schouwburg buildings are located in what became a leafy green suburb of Amsterdam noted for the many white, or mainly white decorative façades of its architecture. The luxuriant Plantage had become an attractive neighbourhood for Jews who had managed to rise up the economic ladder in the late nineteenth century – by 1941, half of its residents were Jewish. Before the war, it had counted many buildings with functions in the Jewish community. The Portuguese Jewish Boys orphanage Aby Yetomim (Father of Orphans) stood at number 80 on Plantage Middenlaan. Further down the same street, opposite Artis Zoo, stood Beth Menucha/ Beth Shalom, the country's largest Jewish home for the elderly. At number 25 stood Talmud Torah, where indigent Jewish boys received free religious and secular education.

At number 11 on Plantage Franschelaan, later renamed Henri Polaklaan, stood another home for the elderly: Ritueel Pension Huize Frank. This residential home, which opened in 1939, was known for its strict observance of the Jewish dietary laws. Further along the same street stood the Portuguese Jewish Hospital and De Burcht van Berlage, headquarters of the diamond workers union (Algemene Nederlandse Diamantbewerkersbond). In 1919, a youth synagogue opened round the corner on Plantage Parklaan, at number 9, run by Beth Yisroel (House of Israel), a Jewish youth movement. There was also a Liberal Jewish community here for a while.

Like Hortus Botanicus, Artis Zoo had long been popular among Jews in the area to meet and enjoy their leisure time. In fact, the Plantage neighbourhood had been attracting pleasure-seekers since the eighteenth century. By the late nineteenth century, it had four theatres and one panorama show. An omnibus route, later a tram, provided regular transport to town.

The Hollandsche Schouwburg

Located at number 24 on Plantage Middenlaan, the Hollandsche Schouwburg was one of those four theatres. Known initially as Artis Schouwburg, it had opened on 5 May 1892 and was renamed two years later. At the top of its ornate façade, replete with pilasters and pediment, were five free-standing statues: Apollo, god of song and music, with four of the muses – Calliope, Melpomene, Terpsichore and Thalia. The pediment featured Venus, goddess of beauty, accompanied by personifications of peace and security and angelic figures illustrating the sibling arts. The exterior was built of brick and stone, subsequently covered with paint, more lately white.

Until 1940, the theatre celebrated many successful seasons – several plays by Herman Heijermans premiered here, and Louis Davids was a popular star. In the 1930s, the venue hosted various Jewish entertainers exiled from Germany and Austria. Given its proximity to the old Jewish quarter, many of its patrons and performers were Jewish. Yet the Hollandsche Schouwburg was a theatre for everyone, still attracting a broad audience well into the first year of the war.

An embroidery by Virginie Keezer-Slijper from the Crèche. Jewish Museum collection.

The Crèche and the Hervormde Kweekschool

Opposite the Hollandsche Schouwburg stood a kindergarten known as the Crèche. It had been founded in 1906 as Vereeniging Zuigelingen-Inrichting for the infant children of observant Jewish mothers who worked away from home, and had first been located on Rapenburgerstraat. The words 'en Kinderhuis' were added in 1919 and the age group widened. In 1924, the Crèche moved into the larger Talmud Torah school building on Plantage Middenlaan, at number 25 – and after the street was renumbered in 1927, number 31. The building was thoroughly renovated, although the study hall on the first floor remained intact. While the Crèche had been founded for Jewish children, it was not exclusive: around seventy percent of the children were Jewish. Many of the parents were market stallholders and seamstresses. In addition to looking after children, this modern, progressive institution also provided courses in childcare. Its two-year programme included lectures by physicians and other experts three nights a week. Trainees also received lessons in Jewish subjects, learning about the rituals and practicalities of Jewish life. The course was well regarded.

This imposing edifice on Plantage Middenlaan, later demolished, was built in 1882 to a design by Isaac Gosschalk, a Jewish architect. The façade featured three double arched windows on the first floor each surmounted by a star of David. Two engaged Greek columns separated the three double windows. At the centre of the roof, a gable featured a stylised star.

The Hervormde Kweekschool, Frank residence (later Frank boarding house for elderly Jews), and 'Zuigelingen-Inrichting en Kinderhuis' kindergarten on Plantage Middenlaan, c. 1930. Amsterdam Resistance Museum collection, unidentified photographer.

Above the double doors at the entrance was the institution's name: Vereeniging Zuigelingen-Inrichting en Kinderhuis. To the right, another door led via an ally to the reception area. It was through this that the children entered. To the right of the central doorway was Henriëtte Pimentel's room: she was appointed director in September 1926. To the left was a room for babies. A dormitory for infants still learning to walk stood at the back of the building. At the centre a stylish circular staircase led to the first floor: there, at the back, was a space for toddlers. Cots were arranged in the dormitory and embroidered decorations on the walls illustrated well-known fairytales, stories and songs. One of those embroideries is shown in the present National Holocaust Museum display. Behind the building, a large garden included sandpits for children to play. The last section of the garden neighboured that of the Hervormde Kweekschool at number 27.

The former Hervormde Kweekschool building dates from 1888. It started as an infants' school. The Dutch Reformed (Hervormde) Church Council bought it in 1906 to set up a teacher-training college on the upper storey. Five years later, the Hervormde Kweekschool took over the whole building. It also had a side entrance, as well as a main front entrance, enabling students

to park their bicycles in the yard at the back. Adjacent to the main entrance was the headmaster's office.

During the war

One day late in the summer of 1941, Betty Oudkerk, a seventeen-year-old Jewish student just starting her training as a childcare worker at the Crèche, stepped from the tram in shock. She had overheard a conversation that had knocked her for six. At work she saw Elly Stein, a colleague. 'Elly,' she said. 'You'll never guess what I heard! I was on the balcony of the tram, and two Germans were standing there talking. One had apparently been on the eastern front and he told the other that there they just shoot Jews and throw them into a pit!' Years later, Elly Stein still remembered that conversation: 'Betty was distraught when she told me. And I said: "Come on girl, that can't be true, that couldn't happen, could it?" It seemed so unreal to us, in that late summer in Amsterdam.'

On 15 September 1941, the Nazis issued a regulation preventing Jews to take part in public and cultural life; Jews were no longer allowed to visit theatres, concert halls, cafés or restaurants. The Hollandsche Schouwburg had been designated an exclusively Jewish location three months earlier, where only Jewish performers appeared to a solely Jewish audience. In October, the Nazis ordered that the theatre's name be altered to Joodsche Schouwburg. Across the road, the Crèche was eventually also reorganised with only Jewish staff caring for only Jewish children.

Henriëtte Pimentel had already taken on Jewish students for the 1941-1942 school year who had been expelled from other institutions elsewhere. On 16 April 1942, only one of the 26 trainees was non-Jewish. She was in her second year and would soon graduate, David Cohen explained in a letter to *Beauftragte des Reichskommissars für die Stadt Amsterdam*. Cohen, one of the two Jewish Council chairs, had been directed to report how many non-Jewish staff were working at the Crèche. The permanent employees, such as qualified childcare workers, a cook and a seamstress, were at that time largely non-Jewish. The Nazis also wanted to know how many non-Jewish children were being looked after there: of the 188 children, nine were not Jewish and fourteen were of mixed parentage. On 28 April, Cohen emphasised the essential role the kindergarten played. Many of the children came from families where the father had been sent to a Jewish labour camp in the Dutch countryside, leaving the mother to help support the family and there being no alternative for the children than the Crèche. In early June 1942, he reported that the various non-Jewish employees had been replaced, and hoped that the non-Jewish staff that remained would be able to stay as long as possible. He stressed that the institute had not been under Jewish Council responsibility for long and that the new employees were still in training. In the end, the last of the non-Jewish staff were also forced to leave.

Umschlagplatz Plantage Middenlaan

On 20 July 1942, the final curtain came down at the Joodsche Schouwburg. It was the end of the playhouse. The Nazis had assigned the theatre an ominous new role: to assemble the women, men and children who had been ordered to report for removal to Westerbork and Vught, and from there to the concentration and extermination camps in Nazi Germany and occupied Poland. The building's name changed again: *Umschlagplatz Plantage Middenlaan*. The first deportees arrived later that same day.

Around 46,000 people are thought to have passed through the Hollandsche Schouwburg. Some reported as ordered. Others were caught at home, in the street, at a care home or in hiding. Many were delivered by bounty hunters. The theatre was often full to bursting. People sat and lay wherever they could: on chairs, on straw, on the wooden floorboards. Sometimes there were fifteen hundred people in a building designed for far fewer. The theatre hall had seated eight hundred, and sanitation facilities were limited. The place became fetid and fusty. People were constantly trying to escape, often aided by Jewish Council employees, yet most were usually recaptured.

Once inside, there was little to do but wait. Some kept their hopes up, others became despondent; all waited the moment of departure to that

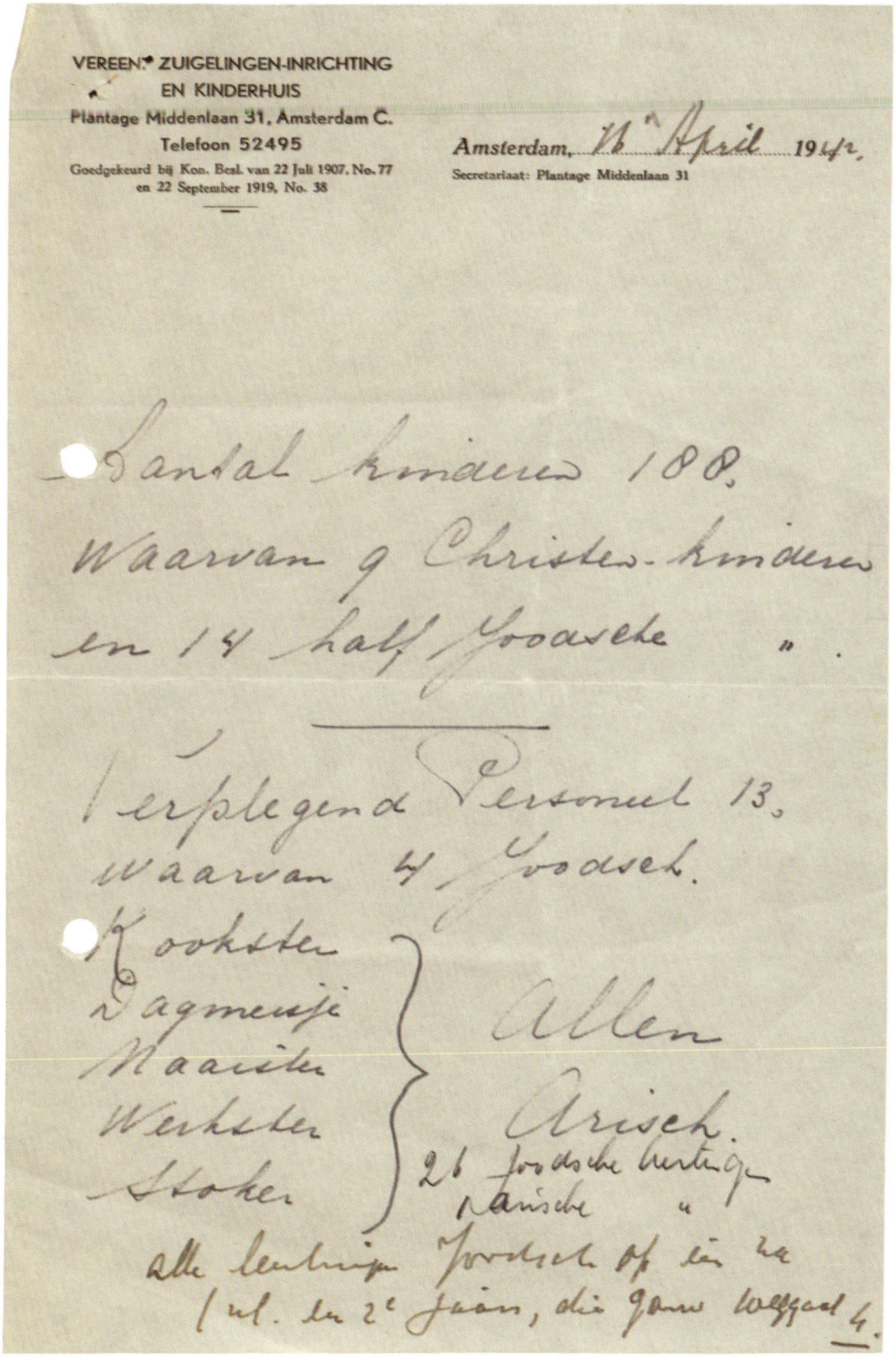

VEREEN.ᵈᵉ ZUIGELINGEN-INRICHTING
EN KINDERHUIS
Plantage Middenlaan 31, Amsterdam C.
Telefoon 52495
Goedgekeurd bij Kon. Besl. van 22 Juli 1907, No. 77
en 22 September 1919, No. 38

Amsterdam, 16ᵉ April 1942.
Secretariaat: Plantage Middenlaan 31

Aantal kinderen 188,
Waarvan 9 Christen-kinderen
en 14 half Joodsche ".

Verplegend Personeel 13,
waarvan 4 Joodsch.
Kookster
Dagmeisje
Naaister
Werkster
Stoker
} Allen Arisch.

21 Joodsche leerlingen
Arische "

Jewish Council registration of the Crèche stating the number of Jewish and non-Jewish children at the kindergarten and likewise the composition of the staff, 16 April 1942. NIOD collection – Jewish Council archive 182, inv. number 27

unknown destination. The uncertainty and fear were too much for some: 'Someone in the infirmary was overcome by panic and six or seven people were needed to hold him down,' wrote Klaartje de Zwarte-Walvisch in her diary.

In October 1942, the Crèche was assigned to take children from the theatre. The youngsters were separated from their parents who were waiting to be deported at the Hollandsche Schouwburg. The Crèche changed from kindergarten to detention centre. While the number of babies, infants and toddlers rose, older children were also sent across the road, up to thirteen years of age. To accommodate them, the reading room was refurnished to make an extra dormitory. And work carried on, as did the training course. The more children arrived from the theatre, the more crowded the Crèche became. When deportations were planned, the children were woken up and walked across the street to the Hollandsche Schouwburg in the evening to be ready to leave with their parents.

Escape from the Crèche

Not long after the Nazis had assigned the Crèche to house the children from the theatre in October 1942, the Jewish Council's administrator at the Hollandsche Schouwburg, Walter Süskind, and his assistants came up with a plan to smuggle Jewish children from the kindergarten into hiding. Adults had already managed to flee the theatre via different routes. Smuggling children out was the next logical step. In January 1943, Süskind met Joop Woortman, a non-Jewish resister, part of the Naamloze Vennootschap group. Together with his assistant Felix Halverstad, Crèche director Pimentel and Woortman, Süskind devised various escape routes. Several childcare workers, including Sieny Kattenburg, Betty Oudkerk, Fanny Philips and Mirjam Cohen, also became involved. Three other resistance groups – Amsterdamse Studenten Groep, Utrechts Kindercomité and Trouw – joined the scheme. They brought the children, all subject to the parents' agreement, to a safe place somewhere in the country. Individuals also played a part, in addition to resistance groups.

Children vanished from the kindergarten in laundry baskets, rucksacks, trashcans, on walks, by tram and later also through the adjacent Kweekschool. At first, the ruses were complex and dangerous. Childcare worker Ines Fellner-Cohn remembers bringing children to Central Station one by one. As the scheme continued, they became more efficient, although the risk was still considerable. Rescuers used nearby buildings – the Jewish

Childcare workers at the Crèche, 1941-1942. Betty Oudkerk (4th from left) recognised herself in the photo. Sieny Kattenburg is seated beside her. Made available by the heirs of Ruth Katz.

community building at Plantage Parklaan 9, and the Jewish Council clothing depot at Plantage Kerklaan 25a – to hand children over to resisters. Some kindergarten staff passed children to resisters on Plantage Franschelaan.

It was around April 1943 that Pimentel approached the Hervormde Kweekschool's director Johan W. van Hulst with a request to use the school's backyard as an extra playground for the children. Van Hulst agreed. Soon after, childcare worker Virrie Cohen asked if she could bring children to sleep in the Kweekschool in the afternoons. Again, the director agreed; he had a spare classroom. They had inadvertently cleared the way for a new escape route: children would be secreted over the fence dividing the two gardens. Resisters would be ready at the side entrance of the school to receive the youngsters and bring them to safety.

The tram stops precisely between the Hollandsche Schouwburg and the Crèche played a vital role in the scheme. When tram 9 heading east to Watergraafsmeer halted in front of the Hollandsche Schouwburg, the guards' view of the Crèche and the adjacent buildings was obscured. Rescuers were then able to walk out into the street taking a child unseen. Tram 9 heading in the opposite direction to Central Station was also used as a cover for flight – that tram stop was slightly further along.

From 25 January 1943, discussions involving the various resistance groups and Pimentel, Süskind and Halverstad were held at number 29, the former boarding house previously run by Izak Frank and his wife Ester Heijmans. Wedged between the kindergarten and the teacher-training college, it had been emptied by the Nazis that day, along with other boarding houses in the

Deportation by tram from the Hollandsche Schouwburg to Muiderpoort station, 1943. Amsterdam Resistance Museum collection, photo by K.F.H. Bönnekamp.

area. Süskind set up his office in the house, now emptied of its boarders, and the rooms were used for childcare workers to live and sleep. This became the hub of the rescue operation.

Final months

On 23 July 1943, two German men in black coats entered the Crèche holding lists. Everyone was ordered to accompany them, although some childcare workers managed to slip away. That night, the Nazis brought Pimentel and deputy director Rebecca Boas, along with various (apprentice) carers and children from the Crèche to the area around Polderweg, near Muiderpoort station. There, with three thousand others, they had to wait for hours to be sent to Westerbork transit camp. In the absence of Henriëtte Pimentel, Virrie Cohen took over as director. She continued the rescue effort with Süskind and Halverstad.

The days leading to the eviction of the last people at the Crèche on 29 September 1943 were hectic. Naamloze Vennootschap resisters tried to get as many children away as they could. In that final week, Virrie Cohen brought fifteen children to Plantage Parklaan 9 and Johan van Hulst was no less busy. Amid the confusion, childcare worker Betty Oudkerk tried to hide a child that hadn't been registered, but was caught. She made a run for it. She went through the adjacent house at number 29 to the Kweekschool attic. There she remained for hours, motionless, before making her way into hiding. All the children who had been caught at the Crèche in that final round-up were brought across the street to the Hollandsche Schouwburg with the various childcare workers. On Friday, 8 October, the children were taken in two buses from Plantage Middenlaan to Panamakade and from there by train to Westerbork.

Mayor Gijs van Hall lighting the *ner tamid* at the unveiling of the memorial, 4 May 1962.
Netherlands Photo Museum collection - Boris Kowadlo, photo by Boris Kowadlo.

The Nazis continued to operate the Hollandsche Schouwburg as a deportation centre for Jews caught in hiding until 19 November 1943. That was the last transport. It seems that they may also have used Frank House at number 29 to accommodate children in that last period. It was later used to store packages meant for Westerbork. Meanwhile the Nazis and collaborators continued to hunt for Jews in hiding, and deportations of Jews from prisons and transit camps went on.

No precise figures are known for the total number of children who passed through the Crèche. It's thought to be between three and five thousand. Around six hundred were rescued.

Deportation centre to memorial

In June 1944, Nationale Hypotheekbank, owners by forfeit, sold the theatre at auction. Two property investors, Harry and Louis Linthorst, bought it and revamped the theatre. After the war they reopened it under a new name: Piccadilly. Under pressure from outraged Jewish survivors, the city council rejected Piccadilly's application for an entertainment license. Various activists, Jews and non-Jews, set up a committee under Sam de Wolff to collect money to buy back the former theatre from its new owners. In 1949, the committee gained possession, and gave the property to the city of Amsterdam on 9 March 1950, on condition that it would never be used for entertainment and a memorial would be installed with a *ner tamid*, an eternal flame. Desolate and unused, the building fell into disrepair. The weathered free-standing statues were taken from the roof for safety. The wooden eaves were also removed either side of the pedestal. To replace the cornice the wall was extended. It was not until 1960 that work started on transforming the Hollandsche Schouwburg into the envisaged site of remembrance and reflection. The plan was developed by architect Jan Leupen of the city's Public Works department, with a *chapelle ardente*, a memorial room, by Leon Waterman, a Jewish architect. In 1962, the time had come: mayor Gijs van Hall lit the *ner tamid*, designed by artist Johan Sterenberg.

Leupen had left the nineteenth-century façade intact, as well as the gable wall where the balustrade had been. The entire exterior was repainted in a warm grey contrasting with the greenish-brown doors. The central three doors gave way to an openwork fence showing passers-by a view of the memorial inside. The former theatre hall was now a lawn and on what had been the stage stood an obelisk on a plinth in the form of a star of David. Behind this, inscribed on the wall, were the words: *In memory of those who were deported from this place, 1940-1945*. Visitors came in through the central hall into the remembrance area, the whole space encompassing the entire ground floor area, and none of the upper floors. Trees and shrubs were planted amid the grass.

In 1993, the memorial received a thorough overhaul. The exterior was repainted and the steel fence was replaced by windows and a doorway. The lawn was paved over and the *chapelle ardente* was replaced by a memorial listing the 6,700 surnames of all the Jewish victims from the Netherlands. On the first floor, a small exhibition was installed about the persecution of Jews in the Netherlands and the story of the Crèche. The former kindergarten had itself been demolished in 1976 to make way for an iconic new structure by architect Aldo van Eyck, to form a refuge for women and mothers with children called Hubertus or Mother House.

Detail of the Hollandsche Schouwburg pediment, with a colour chart on one of the sculptures, 2022. Each paint layer was examined. Colour research and photo by Josefien Tegelaar.

National Holocaust Museum and the Hollandsche Schouwburg

On the site of the former residence and boarding house run by the Franks, a new building has now been erected, designed by architects Uri Gilad and Inez Tan of Office Winhov. They also suppplied the blueprint for the renovation of the adjacent former Hervormde Kweekschool and the Hollandsche Schouwburg. Together, the Kweekschool and the new construction form the National Holocaust Museum. Permanent displays and temporary shows in the museum relate both the local history of the Shoah and the national history of the persecution of the Jews in the Netherlands.

For the restoration of the Hervormde Kweekschool – a place where people showed incredible courage and selflessness – the Jewish Cultural Quarter deliberately asked that elements of the original school be preserved. The panelling, the light fittings and the restored staircase give visitors a sense of being in an old school building. In addition, the shape of the school's historical roof was restored by removing the extension installed in 1953. That had made the building look more like an office complex than an old-fashioned school. The various changes have brought both the interior and exterior more in line with the structure's original identity without actually creating a reconstruction.

The building which had replaced the former Frank residence and boarding house at number 29 in 1961, was demolished in 2020 to make way for an entirely new structure. Here again, the façade follows the contours of the former Frank home, restoring the architectural rhythm of the street. This grand new design is now the entrance to the Holocaust Museum, accentuated by the windows rising above the doorway.
The different format and colour emphasise the history of the house. The architects felt it was important 'to create a canvas to give the imagination space.' Their choice of colour and material are part of that.

The Hollandsche Schouwburg with restored cornice, 2024. Jewish Museum collection, photo by Thijs Wolzak.

◁ **In 1953, the Hervormde Kweekschool roof was extended to create a new top floor. Beside the Kweekschool is the Frank residence, the Crèche, then home to Excelsior laundry and dyers.** Amsterdam municipal archive – Reformed Pedagogical Academy and Hervormde Kweekschool archive.

White, which is such a characteristic colour in the Plantage neighbourhood, played a key role in Gilad and Tan's design. And it also linked to the white exterior of the Hollandsche Schouwburg. In fact, dozens of layers of paint were uncovered during the restoration work on the historic façade, and the colour research revealed greens, browns and yellows to have been the most frequently used. This was no real surprise for the architects, although it did raise the question: which period should their design reflect? It was decided to take the period in which the Hollandsche Schouwburg became a historical monument as a reference point. So the exterior now has a tint that lies closer to the greenish-grey chosen by Jan Leupen: the Hollandsche Schouwburg is and remains a site for remembrance and reflection.

Retaining the structure of each of these historic buildings and emphasising their individual identity through the choice of colour and material, enables local history to come to the fore. And this reinforces for visitors a sense of the successive levels of history that all these buildings embody.

In Remembrance Going Forward

The Shoah's place in postwar Jewish Netherlands

Asjer Waterman

Even though the Second World War ended in 1945 it continues to have a profound impact on Dutch society to this day. That is especially true for the Jewish community in the Netherlands, for whom the memory of the Shoah is always close.

◁ **Bust of Ina Winnik by Max Bueno de Mesquita, terracotta and lacquer, c. 1943.** On loan from Stanley Winnik.

When Ies Winnik emerged from hiding after the war, his life lay in ruins. His wife Sophia and daughter Ina had been taken captive in Amsterdam in the spring of 1943 and killed in Auschwitz in October 1943: the mother at 32, their child at 14 months. His fur shop at Jodenbreestraat 95, where he had lived, had been seized in 1942. He returned to find the Jewish neighbourhood around Waterlooplein, where he was born in 1907, an empty shell. The houses had been ransacked, most of the inhabitants deported and murdered, and the buildings stripped by people searching for wood to burn in their stoves during the winter famine of 1944-1945. Despite it all, Ies was determined to pick up the pieces and carry on. He opened a new fur shop, remarried and raised a son. To keep the memory of his murdered daughter alive, he asked his cousin, artist Max Bueno de Mesquita, to make a bust of Ina. A tangible reminder, so that Ina would always be a part of his new family.

Ies Winnik's decision to commemorate his daughter at home is understandable given the way the culture of remembrance developed in the postwar period. That culture focused in those years principally on Dutch resistance against the Nazis and their accomplices: it was based on the idea that everyone had suffered equally under Nazi rule, without distinction between Jew and non-Jew. The intension was to galvanise the Dutch population into a collective effort to rebuild the country. That left little room for the particular suffering of the Jewish population. Moreover, singling out the Jews as victims would extend the very discrimination the Nazis had practised by treating them as a separate group. Seen from that perspective, a special monument for Jewish victims, a place to remember the personal and collective pain of the Jewish community, seemed inappropriate. Jews were not mentioned as a particular group at national remembrance ceremonies, and the national war archive (Rijksinstituut voor Oorlogsdocumentatie) made no provision for research on the persecution of Jews in the war. The only public war memorial with a specifically Jewish character testified to Jewish Gratitude (Monument voor Joodse Erkentelijkheid), not in recognition of the persecution but in acknowledgement of the efforts of the resistance in defence of Dutch Jews. Most of the Jewish community looked inward to remember the Shoah, preferring to remember those who perished in a Jewish setting: at home, at memorials erected for that purpose at Jewish cemeteries and in synagogue. Ceremonial objects used in synagogue services were donated in memory of family members, like the Torah mantle commissioned by Juda and Jettie Oczeret in honour of their murdered sons, Sallie and Moritz. In this way, people created a space in their own circle to deal with the profound pain felt in the Jewish community.

Even so, there was a lively public interest in what had happened to the Jews. Various publications in the first years after the war focused specifically on the persecution of the Jews during the war. *The Diary of Anne Frank* appeared in 1947, with several reprints following in the 1950s and a play based on the book that premiered in 1956. In 1950, Abel Herzberg's *Kroniek der Jodenvervolging* (Chronicle of the Persecution) was well-received by a broad public. While these volumes gave a sense of the experience of Dutch Jews during the Second World War, they left the national narrative intact. They raised no questions regarding

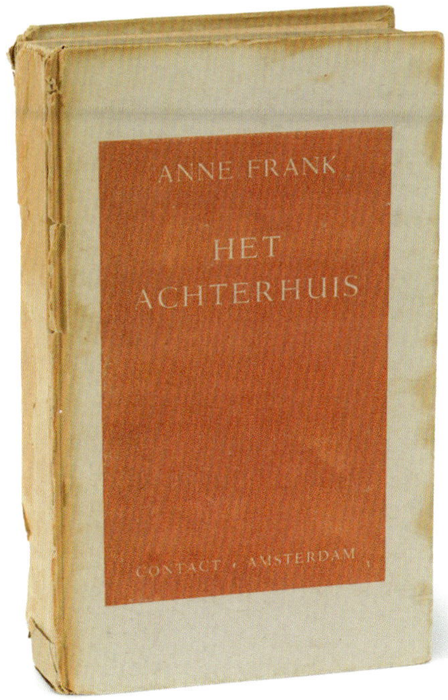

Torah mantle presented by Juda and Jettie Oczeret to NIHS in 1953-1954 in memory of their murdered sons. On loan from Jewish Community of Amsterdam/ NIHS.

the attitude of non-Jews in the Netherlands and the notion that Dutch accomplices had aided and abetted the Nazis. Culpability for the persecution of the Jews lay firmly with the Nazi regime, portrayed as an external phenomenon: it all still slotted neatly into the vision of national unity.

Jews in the Netherlands responded in different ways to this perception of national unity. Some longed for a rapid rehabilitation into Dutch society after years of discrimination and embraced the national remembrance ceremonies. The Jewish Gratitude memorial testifies to the willingness of part of the Jewish community to take the national narrative of gratitude to the resistance on board. Others who took part in national memorials for similar reasons also wished to remember Jewish victims, and did so by participating in specifically Jewish ceremonies on Memorial Day (4 May), or by organising separate memorial events in synagogues or Jewish cemeteries. Whether memorials held by the Jewish community should take place on 4 May or some other day became a contentious issue. For many observant Jews, the religious day of mourning on Tisha b'Av was more appropriate, or even Yom Kippur, the Day of Atonement. That was a day on which special prayers could be said to remember the victims of the Shoah, giving the remembrance a place in an existing Jewish tradition. Since 1946, Jews with an Eastern European background had been marking the start of the Warsaw ghetto uprising on 19 April. Zionist youth movements favoured joining the remembrance of the Shoah on the

◁ **First edition of the diary of Anne Frank, *Het achterhuis*, 1947. Publisher Contact printed 3,000 copies. Reprints soon followed.** Jewish Museum collection.

Hebrew date of 27 Nissan which fell either in April or May. This was the date that the Israeli parliament endorsed by law in 1951. These various memorial dates give a sense of the different ways Jews in the Netherlands endeavoured to form a culture of remembrance. Yet there was no real coherence or unity.

The Hollandsche Schouwburg

Eventually, the monument to the Jews deported from the Netherlands which had remained unbuilt in those first postwar years was realised. After much public debate about what to do with the Hollandsche Schouwburg, a memorial was inaugurated at the former theatre in 1962 in memory of what had befallen the Jews during the Second World War when that building had been an assembly point for those ordered to report for transit to Westerbork. The discussion surrounding the building's purpose had erupted soon after the war. The people who had acquired the building in 1944, were planning to reopen it as a theatre and entertainment venue. To stop them, leading Jewish socialist Sam de Wolff organised a committee of Jews and non-Jews to raise money to buy the building, which they did in 1950. They immediately gave the former theatre to the city of Amsterdam, although views still differed about the function it should serve. Opinions were divided in the Jewish world and the city of Amsterdam refused to take sides. Suggested solutions reflected the disparate views regarding the remembrance of the Shoah in the postwar Jewish community. A proposal to set up an Israel centre in the building to showcase Israel's achievements and to host Zionist activities was vociferously criticised by those who felt it would be inappropriate to celebrate Israel's success in a place so profoundly linked to the Shoah. A less jubilant purpose was needed. Some prominent members of the orthodox Ashkenazi community (Nederlands-Israëlitisch Kerkgenootschap or NIK) argued that the whole edifice should be torn down since a Jewish function for a place so inextricably linked to the Shoah was inconceivable. Yet from Israel's perspective, it was still an ideal location: Zionism as the solution to persecution fitted neatly into the way Israel wished to commemorate the Shoah. After years of animated discussion in which members of the Jewish community spared neither each other or the Israeli ambassador, the city of Amsterdam decided to demolish part of the former theatre and to install a memorial to the Jews deported from the Netherlands in the remaining lobby. The monument to the deported Jews was at last realised.

Flowers at the door of Hollandsche Schouwburg, 1951. NIOD collection.

In 1962 – the year in which the Hollandsche Schouwburg opened as a memorial – the Dutch Zionist union (Nederlandse Zionistenbond or NZB) and the Dutch Jewish community (NIK) hosted a successful joint Jewish commemoration at Minervapaviljoen. Unfortunately, the atmosphere was not so fraternal that participants were moved to repeat the event in later years. When various Jewish youth movements tried again in 1966, the Hollandsche Schouwburg emerged as the natural choice. This came as no surprise. Groups had been gathering outside the building's closed doors every 4 May to mark the day since 1948. When the Hollandsche Schouwburg was opened as a memorial to Jewish victims of the war, representatives of various Jewish organisations had spoken, and in 1965 this was where Jacques Presser presented his long-awaited *Ondergang* – a history of the Destruction of Dutch Jewry, commissioned by Rijksinstituut voor Oorlogsdocumentatie. The site was becoming a memorial to which the Jewish community was beginning to feel increasingly attached.

The youth movements managed to achieve what everyone else had failed to do in 1962: the memorial at the Hollandsche Schouwburg developed into a joint commemoration. Various religious communities and the Zionist union joined the organising panel in the 1970s. Then in 1980, the organisers decided to drop the commemoration of those who died fighting for the state of Israel and to concentrate solely on the victims of the Shoah. The date would continue to be 27 Nissan. The annual Yom Hashoah memorial, which continues to be held in practically the same format as in 1966, had come to fruition. In the 1990s, the building fell under the stewardship of the Jewish Historical Museum which would henceforth also be involved in organising the annual ceremony.

Recognition

It was not until the 1960s that Dutch society gradually came to grasp the extraordinary suffering of the Jewish community. In 1961, an event covered widely in the media was the trial of Adolf Eichmann for war crimes in Israel. A television series by Lou de Jong about the Nazi occupation (*De Bezetting*) also had a huge impact on public opinion, as did Jacques Presser's book, *Ondergang*. The cumulative effect of this growing focus on the Jewish experience made it clear to many that what the average non-Jew in the Netherlands had gone through in the war bore no comparison to what the Jews had endured. Meanwhile, in the 1960s and 70s society was changing and people began to look at the country's history through a different prism. Cultural revolution and the disintegration of traditional social structures undermined the vision of a strong, united Netherlands. The multicultural society emerged as an alternative to the divided society of yesteryear: pluriformity and difference were the new watch words. New testimonies of Jews who had lived through the war were impossible to reconcile with the vision of the Netherlands as a courageous country of resisters that had managed to persevere and forge a path through the war.

With this identification of the Jews as victims came a recognition of the psychological impact the wartime experience had on the Jewish community. The work of Jewish psychiatrists such as Louis Tas, Eddy de Wind and Hans Keilson showed that Dutch Jews were still feeling the effects of the war in their day-to-day life. When legislation was passed in 1973 to provide special pensions to Jewish war victims (Wet Uitkeringen Vervolgingsslachtoffers), a right that resisters had long enjoyed, a milestone was reached in the political recognition of Jews as victims. This acknowledgement led to Jews taking a more visible role in national remembrance ceremonies: Jewish victims of the war were increasingly invited to speak, in fact in 1963 the commemoration had actually been shifted when 4 May fell on a Saturday, since some in the Jewish community would have been unable to attend on Shabbat.

Persecution of the Jews as a national narrative

These parallel developments – social change and public awareness – caused a shift in the national narrative: the war had no longer been a time of resistance and heroism, but of persecution and destruction, with the Shoah as the ultimate example. Auschwitz became a symbol of the potential danger of racism and exclusion that threatened the multicultural

Presentation of Jacques Presser's *Ondergang: de vervolging en verdelging van het Nederlandse Jodendom 1940-1945*; a groundbreaking study on the Holocaust in the Netherlands. IISG collection.

***Metamorfose* by Max Bueno de Mesquita. A triptych about the murder of De Mesquita's sister in Auschwitz. He made the work while a patient of Prof. Jan Bastiaans at Centrum 40-45.** Jewish Museum collection.

fabric of society, and the Shoah became the moral standard for the Dutch. In this new vision, the horrors of war and persecution acquired a role in education and taught us about the way a modern society works. The right way to respond, and the wrong, would henceforth be measured against the history of the Second World War.

This instrumentalization of the history of the persecution of the Jews paved the way to compare the Jewish victims of that time with other victims from the past and the present. In recent decades we have witnessed an ongoing discussion about those who we are commemorating when we stand in silence for two minutes on 4 May. In the 1980s, remembrance ceremonies began referencing current issues that touched on discrimination and exclusion in a wider sense. In the 1990s, ceremonies started paying more attention to individual testimonies of victims of the war, including those of non-Jewish victims such as Sinti and Roma. Then in 2012 The National Committee for 4 and 5 May invited a schoolchild to read a poem about his grandfather's brother who had died fighting for the Waffen-SS on the Russian front at the national commoration ceremony on Dam Square. That the group of victims of the war now apparently also had come to include those who had perpatrated the Shoah caused a commotion in the Jewish community. As a result of this the poem was withdrawn from the programme. This and other incidents made Jews feel that they lost control of their own history: the Shoah had become everyone's property, and the community had lost its say in how its history was used.

The sense of distress that this rebuff caused among Dutch Jews relates in part to the central place that the memory of the Shoah occupies in their identity. For the vast majority, the Shoah is key to their Jewish identity and for many, more so than any other aspect.

It's hardly surprising, therefore, that this is the issue that most unites the different parts of the Jewish community. Jewish commemorative ceremonies are events where Jews of different religious and ideological persuasions come together. Not just at Yom Hashoah ceremonies at the Hollandsche Schouwburg, but at other memorial events marking Kristallnacht, organised by Centraal Joods Overleg, the National Holocaust Commemoration at Wertheimpark – previously Auschwitz Remembrance – and 4 May ceremonies with a traditionally strong Jewish component like the event on Apollolaan in Amsterdam. And then there are the countless small-scale events such as the ceremony at the Jewish Resistance memorial or the commemoration of the 1942 round-up at Hollandia

Page from the *Boek der tranen* (*Book of tears*) commemorative album, compiled in 1945 in memory of the Jewish employees deported from Hollandia-Kattenburg cloth mill. It contains a photo of almost every employee. Jewish Museum collection, on loan from Herdenkingscomité Hollandia-Kattenburg.

Kattenburg cloth mill where 367 Jewish employees and their families were taken and deported. It's at these ceremonies that the Jewish community feels a sense of solidarity and unity. The memory of the Shoah has become a binding factor unifying the community, while at the same time it fosters a sense of alienation from Dutch society as a whole.

Today

Interest in the Shoah has grown in recent decades, and the memory of the Second World War has acquired more of a national character than ever before. It was as recently as 2012 that the Auschwitz Committee's request to attach the predicate 'national' to the Wertheimpark ceremony was denied by the secretary of state for Health, Welfare and Sport. The addition has since been approved and the ceremony is now one of three national memorials, alongside the National Remembrance on 4 May and the National Remembrance on 15 August for the Dutch victims who fell in the former colony of Dutch East Indies. The Names Memorial in Amsterdam is a national monument too, and

Uitgave van het Amsterdams 4 en 5 mei comité, Mediamatic en Partizan Publik, in het kader van het project Joodse Huizen (4 mei) en de tentoonstelling Pièce de Resistance (24 april – 26 juni 2011)

IS DIT JOUW HUIS?

Staat jouw huis in de onderstaande lijst? Hierin staan de 21.662 adressen waar circa 61.700 Joodse Amsterdammers woonden die in de Tweede Wereldoorlog zijn vermoord. Woon je in een huis uit de lijst en wil je hen herdenken? Dan kun je op 4 mei de poster uit deze bijlage voor het raam hangen. Of een bezoek brengen aan **www.joodsmonument.nl/huizen**

Publication for the Jewish Houses project, 4 May 2011, distributed as a supplement with copies of *Het Parool* newspaper. Jewish Museum collection.

the Holocaust Museum is also national: both having received financial backing from the municipality and central government. At the same time, national initiatives are in place to give greater visibility to the history of the Shoah and to keep the memory of that history alive with projects such as Stolperstein pavement memorials, *Theater na de Dam* performances at the annual 4 May ceremonies, Open Jewish Houses and the *Parool* newspaper's 'Is this your house' 2011 campaign to show the houses from which Jews were deported in Amsterdam.

Meanwhile, these initiatives have also garnered unwelcome responses from various sections of society; plans for the construction of the National Names Memorial were opposed in the neighbourhood, both when it was initially proposed for Wertheimpark and when its alternative location on Weesperstraat was selected. Similarly, the placing of pavement memorial plaques has also met with resistance. Some people resent being reminded of the Shoah every day. Recent decades have seen the advent of Holocaust fatigue – a sense that it's time for these constant reminders of the Shoah to end – while fears have been expressed that young people know less and less about what happened in the Second World War. Paradoxically, we find ourselves in a situation in which social engagement with the history of the Second World War is declining at a time when initiatives to keep that history alive and combat ignorance about the Shoah among young people are increasing.

Video installation in which (grand)children of survivors recount the role the persecution and murder of Jews, Sinti and Roma plays in their own lives. Lalla Weiss is daughter of Sinti leader Hannes Weiss. Production Shosho.

Nonetheless, the Second World War still remains a litmus test in discussions about right and wrong, giving it a central place in our collective consciousness. That this history will continue to play a role in Dutch society seems incontrovertible. For the Jewish community, the way its memory is expressed, and how the Jewish experience and consequent suffering are acknowledged in this context, will largely determine its relationship with Dutch society in general. With the opening of the National Holocaust Museum, an institution has come into being that will continue to focus attention on the persecution of the Jews in the Netherlands from start to finish.

Stolperstein pavement memorial commemorating Annie Haagens-Roos and Lion Haagens. Jewish Museum collection.

HIER WOONDE
LION HAAGENS
GEB. 1895
GEDEPORTEERD 1942
UIT WESTERBORK
VERMOORD 28.8.1942
AUSCHWITZ

The Shoah in the Museum

Choices in a presentation on mass murder

Annemiek Gringold

Creating a museum to present a complicated, difficult history like that of the Holocaust requires the trust of those directly involved and needs curators and designers to take clear-cut choices. We identified the need to retain the human scale amid an overwhelming history as our main idea, with openness and transparency as our leading principles.

◁ **The Hollandsche Schouwburg entrance, 2024.** Jewish Museum collection, photo byThijs Wolzak.

In the course of the Second World War, Nazis and their collaborators killed around six million Jewish men, women and children. This is known as the Holocaust. The Hebrew term is Shoah, which means catastrophe. Its history is horrific and its impact on Dutch society was huge.

The Shoah took place throughout Nazi-controlled Europe, including the occupied Netherlands. Indeed, a greater percentage of the Dutch Jewish community perished than in any other West European country. The two buildings of the National Holocaust Museum, Hollandsche Schouwburg and Hervormde Kweekschool, along with the Frank family home, played a prominent part in that history. Today, the two buildings, both originally designed for entirely different functions, have been converted into a museum and memorial dedicated to that history and are themselves the main feature of the presentation. Other museums in the Netherlands are also dedicated to the Second World War and the Shoah: Anne Frank House, for example, Overloon War Museum, Westerbork Memorial Centre and Amsterdam's Resistance Museum. The National Holocaust Museum is the first museum with a comprehensive presentation of Jewish life before the Shoah, the persecution and murder during the years of occupation, and the processing and aftershocks of the Shoah in Dutch society after liberation. It is also the first museum in the Netherlands with a distinct Jewish character where the permanent exhibition depicts the devastation within the Jewish community.

Creating a Holocaust museum

Developing a presentation about a difficult subject like the Shoah requires both a well-argued premise and sensitivity in form and content. Every idea, every aspect of the design and every word has to support the museum's vision, which is to enable audiences to observe and understand, to consider and commemorate and to encourage involvement and good citizenship: observe, reflect and act. These aspects of visitor experience are the criteria against which we test the elements that we have brought together to create the museum. Exhibits, texts, film clips, photos, audio segments and witness testimony, the historic buildings themselves, the layout, design and language, colour and light: they all combine to form a narrative. They all come together to convey information about the persecution, the mass murder and who made it possible. At the same time, the museum also examines other perspectives. This article looks at the premise, the design and the choices made in the development of the National Holocaust Museum and Hollandsche Schouwburg presentations.

First generation quotes

One recurring element is the use of quotations, written and spoken by those who were there. These enable victims and survivors to connect directly with the audience. For example, at the entrance to the former theatre visitors read: 'it happened, therefor it can happen again; that is the essence of what we have to say'. A statement from Primo Levi, who, as a 24-year-old Italian Jew, was deported to Auschwitz in 1944 and survived.

Levi's message brings together two key perspectives. First, that of the persecuted, specifically the few who somehow survived the Shoah. Those survivors, on whose behalf Levi speaks, who lost everything, their family and loved ones, their home and all they owned, their dignity and their future, they say just one thing: watch out! Based on their memories and experiences, they issue a warning: what happened to them can happen again. The other perspective contained in Levi's words is also about the danger that the same crimes can be committed again, but it engages the perspective of the perpetrators. It can happen again, and therefore, it can also be prevented. In certain circumstances, events and choices can lead to mass murder, to genocide. The museum plays its part in preventing a repetition by disseminating knowledge about what happened, about perpetrators and their accomplices, about motives and circumstances. Levi's words exhort visitors to be alert and to think about the Shoah, about the possibility of it happening again and our responsibility to ensure it never does.

The quote from Levi is not the only one. Quotations of those directly involved are incorporated into the texts accompanying the exhibits and projections. The museum maker, as the sender of the narrative, gives those who lived through the war the opportunity to speak. It's their history and it's important that they get to tell their story directly to the visitor. Some quotes help people to reflect and find inspiration, others inspire amazement and curiosity. Filmed eye-witness testimony also appears in the presentation. Visitors can listen to personal memories seated at a screen. Watching survivors testify, seeing and hearing them speak, leaves an indelible impression on the audience. As the generation of survivors gradually disappears, there will soon be no one left to tell the story first-hand. So the museum is a place where witnesses can make their recollections part of the narrative. Visitors can watch their full testimony in the museum's Resource Centre. It's one of the few opportunities to experience their narrative so intimately.

The buildings

The commission to the architects at Office Winhov was to make the museum building light and transparent. Since the building served as a school during the war, the idea was to preserve that original layout in the building's new form. Also on the list of requirements was that the Hollandsche Schouwburg renovations show respect for the building's history. A key requirement was for both buildings to preserve an unbroken visual connection from the street to the space at the back. The line of sight from the street to the wall over which children were smuggled during the war, and the sight of the original proscenium through the old theatre windows across the road reinforces the impression of these buildings as historic locations. History happened here. These visual effects also emphasise the museum as an open location for everyone to visit, revealing everything and leaving no taboo unspoken.

The materials for the construction and displays were chosen carefully. While other Holocaust and Second World War museums are generally designed in shades of grey, with rough surfaces and reconstructions of original architecture to evoke a historical atmosphere and location, we took a different approach. This presentation is not an immersive experience where visitors wander through a stage set. The Shoah was a period of extreme indignity and injustice: to recreate a scene portraying the humiliation they suffered here would be an affront to the people who lived through it. Therefore, the design and layout present each object with respect. Visitors engage with the history through the objects and the empathetic narrative.

Because the events took place in broad daylight, the architects created a museum that radiates light. Wherever possible sunlight illuminates the interior, while the view through the windows keeps visitors aware of the location and the visual proximity of the events of the period for everyone who was there. The materials and colours match the layout of the old school building. The architects have differentiated the functional elements of the former teacher-training school and the adjacent Frank family home in subtle ways. This reminds

The restored Kweekschool staircase, 2023. Photo by Raymond van Mil.

viewers at each turn that the site itself is intimately linked to the history. Moreover, the atmosphere of the interior, the school corridors, classrooms and the restored staircase excite the curiosity and active involvement of visitors.

Designing the display

The museum presentation – *The Netherlands and the Shoah* – begins on the second floor of the former teacher-training school. After a short introduction and tour of the rooms, the visitor follows the route downstairs to ultimately view the rooms about deportation and murder.
A central hall on the two floors provides the opportunity to deviate from the main route. There's one place where that's not possible: the room containing a display of personal objects relating to stories that illustrate the various paths which led from arrest to transit camp. There the museum route and spatial design emphasise the impossibility of escape once caught in the Nazi web.

The Jews in the Netherlands before the war were far more than what the Nazis made of them: victims. The Nazis may have persecuted and murdered, but the Jews of the Netherlands had also lived their life in those years. Many Jewish families had resided in the Netherlands for centuries, mostly in Amsterdam. They were part and parcel of the country's society and culture, they worked in shops, served in the army, painted, practised medicine. When we show their history, we try to convey a sense of their life and not just the cruel fate that awaited them. Because that would be a disservice to their memory. Presenting them as recognisable people who lived a life, no different from people we know today, reduces the distance that visitors would otherwise feel. Personal stories make history relatable and encourage visitors to find out more, to get curious.

With that in mind, the museum worked together with OPERA Amsterdam and Studio Louter to develop a unique design concept: the so-called forget-me-not installations. There are nineteen of these in the presentation, introducing our audience to nineteen Jews who lived during the Shoah and were murdered. Placed on slender, sometimes slanted legs, positioned slightly off-center, the forget-me-not

Personal stories about the route to the transit camp, for visitors too there's only one way to proceed. Jewish Museum collection, photo by Thijs Wolzak.

installations display the vulnerability of individuals in that overwhelming, unforgiving inferno. Each installation is different in shape and material, representing a unique person in an ode to their existence. An object and photo is introduced by a short text on the support. The photo gradually morphs into a colour image and back again to the black-and-white original. And as the visitor approaches, the exhibit is subtly lit. The presence of someone interested in their existence brings their memory into the spotlight. They are not forgotten. And the audience gets to know them by listening to their story. Forget-me-nots are placed in the various presentation rooms, and the personal items relate in each case to the featured theme.

The lives of these nineteen Jews from around the country, each with their own experience, can't convey a complete history of the Shoah in the Netherlands. To do that, the museum would need over 140,000 stories. To show the devastating intricacy and complexity of the segregation and robbery, of the discrimination and deportation the designers employed a different concept. More than any other country under Nazi rule, in the Netherlands the perpetrators weaved a quasi-legal fabric of regulations and edicts to prepare and implement the Shoah. With one regulation after another, with notices and instructions, the Nazis created a legal structure that robbed Jews of all rights. The first orders came immediately after the Nazis took over, and

A forget-me-not installation shows film images of Daatje Frank. Her doll was saved. Jewish Museum collection, photo by Thijs Wolzak.

a steady stream continued until 1945. In a large part of the presentation, the visitor is surrounded by legal texts and executive orders that describe the process of detection, segregation, discrimination, impoverishment, exploitation, identification, deportation and murder. The writing covers metre after metre of wall, evoking the pervasive sense of oppression, the arbitrary dismissal of legal rights and the cumulative restrictions. The walls expose the enormity of the wrongdoing. Indeed, all these regulations showing how thoroughly the Nazis organised their crimes, illustrate the vulnerability and the need to protect the rule of law. For visitors, the display of legalised injustice shows how vital it is that we defend the constitutional values that protect our rights, and those of every minority.

Objects

Alongside the forget-me-not installations and the wall texts, the presentation also features numerous objects, documents, photos and films: around 2,500 exhibits come from dozens of museum collections in the Netherlands and abroad. The back-lit blow-ups of photos in the display trace a chronological line, together with the scenographic projections of film fragments.

Material objects make the history tangible and at the same time personal. Everyday objects become key heritage carriers through their origin, their use and the accompanying stories. Like the nine-year-old Berthold Barenholz's simple checked shirt. He hid under a floor when two Dutch bounty hunters came to fetch him after his hide-out had been betrayed. They shot through the wooden floorboards, wounding the boy; the holes are visible in the shirt. His parents had kept in touch with a relative in Westerbork through Friedrich Weinreb, a Jew they were relying on. Tragically, the Nazis found out. The family were caught, survived deportation to Bergen-Belsen and liberated over a year after their capture at Tröbitz, in Germany. The boy was still wearing that same shirt; he had nothing else. The garment links that whole series of events. It illustrates the desperate hope of those who hid, their betrayal, the shelter and the capture, deportation and survival. The historical value of a single object is immense, linking all these stories. Its value in the museum lies in its recognisable, everyday immediacy, bringing visitors closer to history, enabling them to empathize, inspiring them to act.

Other objects are less directly recognisable for a broad audience; these symbolise the Jewish identity of their original owners. A tallit (prayer-shawl), a Chumash (Pentateuch) and a mezuzah (doorpost case) are all traditional Jewish objects. Other specifically Jewish objects include Hebrew textcards and a wedding announcement in the form of an Esther scroll, whose purpose is more secular. All these items are not just part of the history of the Shoah, they also

The anti-Jewish regulations on the wall are written in Futura, a letter type designed in 1927 and occasionally used in Nazi Germany for publications.
Jewish Museum collection, photo byThijs Wolzak.

convey a sense of Jewish tradition and custom, Jewish culture, and the identity of their owners. In addition, this being a national museum, objects have been selected from the entire country. And because the country was still a colonial power during the Second World War, displays also throw a spotlight on the Dutch territories.

Many objects from the Second World War period are now extremely fragile. The scarcity of paper meant that the quality was often poor. Cloth too: many items which had been worn through were not preserved with care. Objects made of wood, metal or celluloid were easily damaged. Almost all these exhibits have been cleaned. To display them properly and responsibly, some have had to be restored, sometimes to stabilise them. In fact, material heritage from the Shoah that has suffered wear and tear is all the more powerful if it isn't nicely restored and polished and retains the traces of its turbulent past. That's why restorers have often intervened as little as possible, sufficient only to preserve the object and enable its proper display.

The shirt of Berthold Barenholz. On loan from the Barenholz family.

Textiles were restored in the museum storage depot and the restoration studios. Jewish Museum collection, photo by Nienke Fonk.

Language

Beside the concepts, designs and objects, language also plays a crucial role in the National Holocaust Museum. First and foremost, the use of the word Shoah in addition to Holocaust. Word choices are an even more sensitive issue when it comes to terms used by the Nazis themselves. They often used euphemisms and terms that denigrated and dehumanised Jews. They used the word transport, for example, rather that deport, which here reflects the agency of the Nazi perpetrators. Nazis also used other words to insult their victims, and at the same time make their instructions appear benign. Bureaucrats for example used the word evacuation instead of deportation. So the transfer of Jews to concentration camps would appear

The theme texts are numbered and show visitors where they are in the presentation. Jewish Museum collection, photo by Thijs Wolzak.

honest and legitimate. In the museum, language, both written and spoken, is the principal means of communication with the audience. The museum texts encourage visitors to observe, reflect and act. The writers have chosen their words carefully, raising questions, highlighting details and sharing different perspectives. And the various texts are in a hierarchical order. The main thematic texts are short, and numbered one to twelve. That gives readers a sense of where they are in the presentation and of what's coming, enabling them to skip sections if they want.

Confrontational

Museums about the Shoah often provide a space for visitors to stop and reflect, a place to sit and contemplate, or pay their respects at a memorial. This history naturally leaves visitors feeling upset. Here at the National Holocaust Museum, many of the displays are emotional and shocking and may lead visitors to wonder about their own assumptions and their responsibilities. Extremely confrontational topics are aired here, such as collaboration, the actions of perpetrators and the Jewish Council. The museum deals with these themes on a human scale. With pictures of individual perpetrators in everyday settings, rather than in a typical Nazi context. They appear as ordinary people. The idea is to show visitors that it was ordinary people with ordinary lives who committed these crimes, so there's no reason to imagine that it can't happen again. The Jewish Council's history is not about perpetrators. It remained a hot topic until long after the war. Views and opinions about the organisation range from sympathetic criticism

Writing desk by David Cohen. Jewish Museum collection.

to angry condemnation. Some of these sentiments are aired in a display around the desk of David Cohen, who chaired the Jewish Council. Views, not facts, help visitors form their own ideas about the Jewish Council after having seen the whole presentation.

Appeal

Visitors leave the presentation with an appeal ringing in their ears: Now that you know. Don't forget. Don't be indifferent! This accompanies the last of the forget-me-not installations showing three photos of an unidentified family and their last words: 'Don't forget us!'

In *The Netherlands and the Shoah*, the museum encourages visitors to reflect, to value their good intentions and their sense of responsibility. The gardens, replete with artworks, educational programmes, contemplative spaces and a museum café offer an opportunity for conversation and make this a museum in every sense. The opening of the museum in 2024 in the presence of the Dutch monarch Willem-Alexander comes 79 years after the end of the Second World War.

It happened here

Searching on a thin line

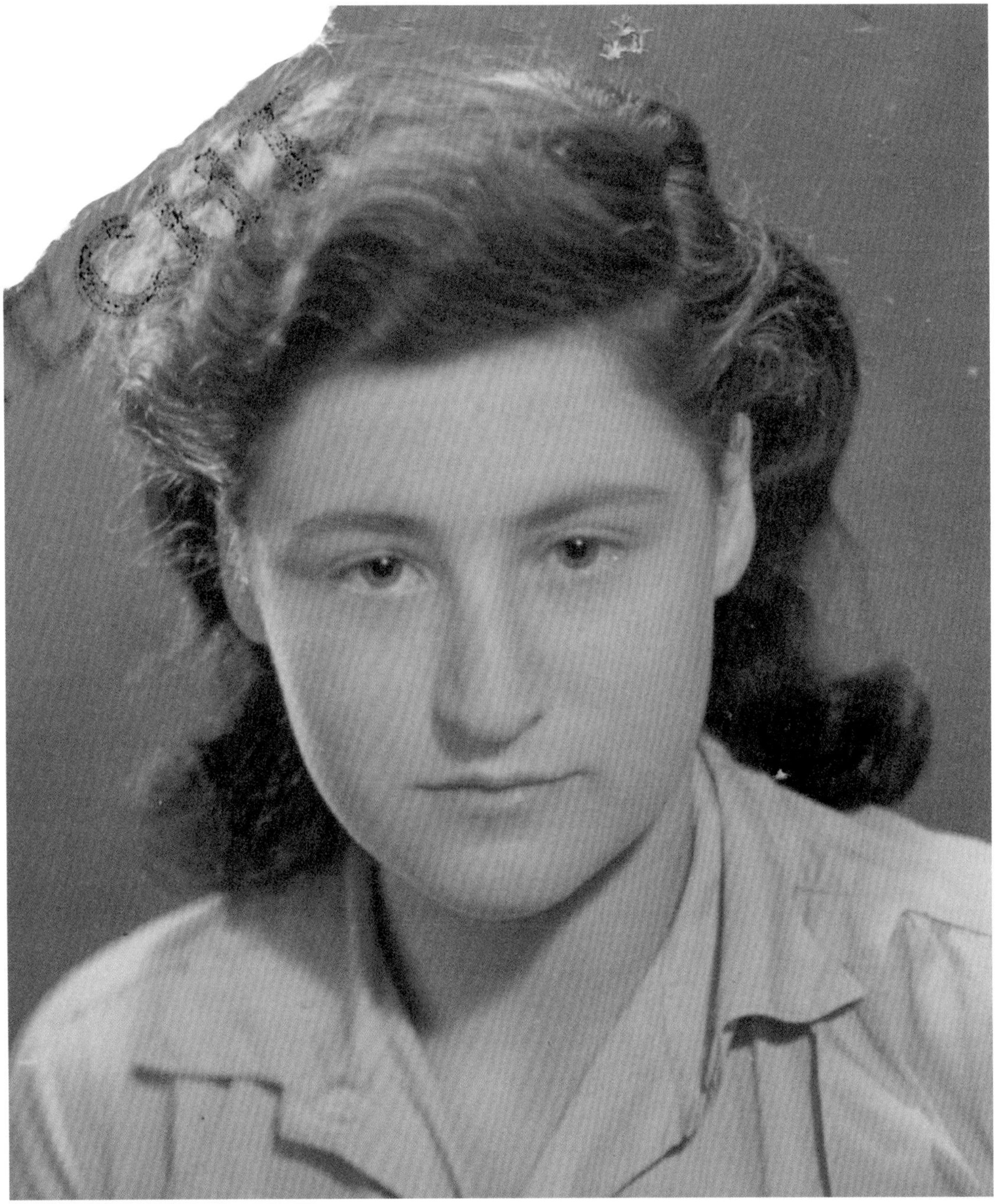

Astrid Sy

The buildings of the former Hervormde Kweekschool and the Hollandsche Schouwburg are the National Holocaust Museum's principal exhibits. The museum tells the history of the Shoah at the place it happened. For museum visitors, that brings history challengingly close.

◁ **Rosetta Musaph-Andriesse, aged around fifteen.** R. Musaph-Andriesse collection.

'It happened here, in this neighbourhood, in this city, and in this country. And you still smell it as you enter the theatre, I still smell it.'
Rosetta Musaph-Andriesse

Rosetta Andriesse was almost sixteen in 1943, when her hiding place was discovered and she was taken to the Hollandsche Schouwburg. Decades later she describes the chaos. People crying. Children screaming. The fear was palpable, and the sense of helplessness. She still remembers how she hid in the prop room under the stage. How she was smuggled across the road to the Crèche. How she lost hope and longed to be with her parents, who were already in Westerbork. In the end, Rosetta was deported to Bergen-Belsen and she survived. She recollected those experiences in 2014. It happened here, in this neighbourhood. You smell it as you enter the theatre.

Prisoners look out of the windows at the Hollandsche Schouwburg's backyard. They can also be seen climbing over the fence to a next house. The fire escape under the window leads to the street, July 1942. NIOD collection - Beeldbank WO2/M. van Nobelen, photo by Lydia Riezouw.

For thousands of Jews, the Hollandsche Schouwburg was where their deportation began, via Westerbork or Vught to the concentration and extermination camps in Nazi Germany and occupied Poland. Children were separated from their parents and held across the road at the Crèche until their departure. An estimated 46,000 Jews were deported via the Hollandsche Schouwburg. Some managed to escape with help from Jews employed there for various tasks. Around six hundred children were smuggled from the Crèche into hiding. Many of them through the garden of the adjacent Hervormde Kweekschool, a teacher-training college.

Rosetta's words can be understood in different ways. Witnesses have testified that the stench at the Hollandsche Schouwburg was overpowering. Hundreds of people crammed into the theatre hall, sometimes days on end. No fresh air, no daylight. Musty, fear-laden, with insufficient sanitary facilities: the conditions were demeaning.

Yet Rosetta's words are a metaphor too. A prominent street in Amsterdam with a thriving playhouse, a prestigious kindergarten and a well-respected teacher-training college – the Hervormde Kweekschool – all inextricably linked to the persecution of the Jews. For the survivors after the war, it would always take

Plantage Middenlaan with the National Holocaust Museum and the neighbouring Hubertus House designed by architect Aldo van Eyck, which replaced the earlier Crèche. Jewish Museum collection, photo by Thijs Wolzak.

Introductory film about the history of the Hollandsche Schouwburg, shown in the entrance hall. Jewish Museum collection, photo by Thijs Wolzak.

them back to the suffering they had endured: waiting in inhumane conditions, families torn apart, children separated and confined. For most people this was where their journey to destruction began. Whenever Rosetta comes to the Hollandsche Schouwburg, she relives what happened here. For her, the Hollandsche Schouwburg and Plantage Middenlaan reek of the Shoah.

Buildings as museum objects

Being at a historical location adds an extra dimension to the historical experience for people visiting the museum. It happened here, as Rosetta says. The veil that divides past from present is thinnest in a place like this. You can see the history. You can touch it. The National Holocaust Museum's location is no coincidence. The museum's home is in the Hervormde Kweekschool. And the National Holocaust Museum presentation continues in the Hollandsche Schouwburg display rooms which make a visit to this historical monument a profound experience, giving audiences a sense of the place they are visiting, of what happened here and why the location is so important. It starts at the Hollandsche Schouwburg as visitors enter. Billboards on the exterior wall with photos and posters refer directly to the building's original purpose: once a theatre for everyone, as Jews were increasingly segregated, a Jewish theatre, then a deportation centre and in the end, a memorial.

The history of the Hollandsche Schouwburg and the Hervormde Kweekschool is a story about people: it encapsulates the worst and the best of humanity. The Nazi regime and Dutch collaborators saturated the Hollandsche Schouwburg in guilt. Rescues by Jews who worked at the theatre and the Crèche, aided by Kweekschool staff and non-Jews in resistance groups, made these buildings places of hope, courage and solidarity.

It's this combination of historic location and the experience of real people that gives it such a powerful impact. Because presenting personal testimonies where the events happened enables audiences to empathise with the experiences of people in history. Especially with a history like that of the Shoah. That's why the Hollandsche Schouwburg and the former Kweekschool are perhaps the most important objects in the National Holocaust Museum. That combination of historic location and personal testimony is the premise on which the layout of the buildings is based.

Reconstructing history

While the buildings are anchored in the local history of the Shoah, almost nothing of the interior remains to recall the past. The theatre balconies and the red plush seating are gone. Visitors can't see where Rosetta hid under the stage, or where the tables stood with typewriters ready to register and record. The Crèche was demolished almost fifty years ago. Only the old staircase and a few mural tiles in the side entrance recall the Kweekschool's original function as a college. Some of the classrooms have survived. Yet these look nothing like they did in the war. Even the old Kweekschool garden, where children were passed from the Crèche to the resisters who smuggled them out, has changed irrevocably over the years.

Both the renovated buildings have been designed to bring audiences closer to the history of the place and the experiences of those who lived through the wartime events, yet without creating replicas. Historical reconstructions would never succeed in visualising what actually happened and would inevitably be historically incorrect. Placing reconstructed cots in the Kweekschool classroom would never truly convey the traumatic experience of the children who had to sleep there. The conditions in the theatre hall as described by people who were there are also impossible to replicate. Is it even possible to reenact fear? Chaos? Abuse? Smell?

Moreover, it's impossible to say with absolute certainty what the buildings looked like inside. Few historical sources survive from the time of the deportations. Some of the testimonies seem contradictory. The situation also changed over time. Were childcare workers able to pass freely between the gardens of the Kweekschool and the Crèche or did they lift the rescued children over the fence? Were the seats in the theatre hall fixed in place, or shifted to the side? Much of the added detail is speculative and superfluous.

We have enough evidence to get a sense of the history of the Shoah from accounts based on reliable research, using reliable images from an array of testimonies relating to these historical locations. How is that achieved in the two buildings?

The Hollandsche Schouwburg – a visit on various levels

The Hollandsche Schouwburg is first and foremost a historical monument, a commemorative site. People still visit every day to remember the victims of the Shoah. Subtly integrated museum elements enhance the visiting experience on different levels. In the entrance foyer an introductory film playing on 35 screens tells audiences about the building's history. Animations help them imagine moments for which we have no historical images. But the sober design, the use of dark and light, shadows and simple floorplans give visitors ample opportunity to use their imagination.

In the former theatre hall, specially designed luminous glass teardrops show the faces of people who were confined there: Jews of varying ages from around the Netherlands. Placed at intervals along the side walls, they invite visitors to listen to their recorded testimonies. Some are about rescue, others describe the violence and the panic. Suicide is another painful subject, as is a parent's decision to let a rescuer take their child. Frieda Elburg-van Dam from Groningen explained in an interview after the war how she

Each glass drop features a picture and illuminated animation. Visitors can listen to personal testimony about prisoners' experiences. Jewish Museum collection, photo byThijs Wolzak.

One of two photos in the contemplative garden at the Hollandsche Schouwburg. In 1942, Greetje Velleman was standing in the theatre backyard when she waved to her non-Jewish friend Lydia Riezouw who took this photo. NIOD collection - Beeldbank WO2/M. van Nobelen, photo by Lydia Riezouw.

gave her daughter, just a few days old, to the resistance. 'I saw her coming. I gave Lineke to her and watched as she took Lineke to the tram. I had no idea where she was going. Yes, I wanted to scream... All I knew was that this was the only way to save my child.' Now that the last generation of survivors is ever fewer in number, these eye-witness testimonies are all the more crucial. Those who didn't survive are also represented. Recordings of diary extracts and letters bring their Hollandsche Schouwburg experience painfully close.

Listening to the eye-witness testimonies, visitors are naturally drawn to the memorial obelisk surrounded by the remains of the proscenium. Engraved on the memorial wall are the words: 'In memory of those who were deported from here.' Having learned about the history of the Hollandsche Schouwburg, having heard the personal testimonies, here visitors can remember the victims and relate to the information they have digested since they entered. Towards the rear, a garden provides a tranquil retreat in which to reflect further. A visit to experience on different levels: informative, empathetic, commemorative, reflective.

Henriëtte Pimentel garden at the National Holocaust Museum. This is where the Crèche and Kweekschool gardens meet. Jewish Museum collection, photo byThijs Wolzak.

The Kweekschool – the children and their rescuers

In the former teacher-training college the history of the Crèche is the central theme. That history, which is discussed more extensively elsewhere in this volume, is told in various ways. A glass veranda looks out onto the Henriëtte Pimentel garden, named after the resister and director of the Crèche.
A feature of the garden is the long, tall wall that divides it from the garden of the former Crèche.

The glass veranda is about the children and what they experienced. Many had little idea what was happening, where their parents were and why they were smuggled away by complete strangers. They had no control over their fate, they were just children. The extreme helplessness and danger they felt would stay with them all their life, as a film shows in which five former kindergarten children share their memories. Memories of the Crèche, of their escape, hiding, and how their wartime experiences affected them later through childhood and adulthood.

Visitors have a view of the wall marking the property boundary of the Crèche. Inside, they can learn more about the rescue of Jewish children. Jewish Museum collection, photo by Thijs Wolzak.

This film tells the story in loose fragments because that's how children remember: sometimes clear and sharp, other times full of gaps, distorted, magnified, colourful or darkly sinister. Five different stories, each full of loneliness and helplessness: the Jewish child vaguely aware they were not supposed to exist. Staying close to the recollections, without much context or explanation, gives a tangible sense of their lonely, helpless predicament. Rosie Colthof recalls the moment she escaped from the Crèche: 'I think I just let it all happen. After all, what could I do? There was no way I could object.'

The history of the Crèche is one of tremendous sadness: children incarcerated, separated from their parents, waiting to be allowed back across the road, and then deported. A fault line with detention, deportation and death on one side, and freedom, safety and life on the other. Symbolised by the wall that once divided the Crèche and the Kweekschool gardens. *'I don't dream of the children who were saved; in the mirror of my memory, I see a line of children departing via the Crèche's front door, crossing the street to be deported,'* Virrie Oudkerk-Cohen recalled in an interview for *Vrij Nederland* magazine in 1986. Her words describing the drama that unfolded at the Crèche with such precision, are displayed on the wall above nine life-size photos of children who didn't make it. Such as Willem Vega: murdered at the age of three at Sobibor, together with his brother Maurits aged five, and his four-year-old sister Henriëtte. Or Koenraad Huib Gezang – who they called Remi the orphan: just one year old when he was killed at Sobibor. The photos of the children lead to director Henriëtte Pimentel, depicted in the tenth photo holding her pet dog Bruni.

From the veranda and the Henriëtte Pimentel garden, visitors trace the path that the rescuers took as they brought the children across the former schoolyard to the side entrance. The paving, some still from the period, is a reminder that this was once a school. Jewish children

Lifesize photos of children in the Henriëtte Pimentel garden. All the children shown here were deported from the Crèche and murdered. Jewish Museum collection, photo by Thijs Wolzak.

The Kweekschool's former side entrance. An escape route for children from the Crèche. Jewish Museum collection, photo by Thijs Wolzak.

Classroom 1 explains the stages for the rescue of a child from the Crèche. NV resistance group found people willing to hide Jews. Here NV resisters Gerard Musch (l) and Koos Postuma (r) appear with children in hiding. Jewish Museum collection.

walked here in those days, smuggled from the Crèche, led out by their carers. No photo or film was ever made. But the moment of their escape would remain etched in the children's memory. Their words are projected on the wall tiles, their footsteps leading to the front door, to a life in the shadows, in hiding.

During the deportations, the Kweekschool director Johan van Hulst emptied a classroom to give children from the overcrowded Crèche a place to sleep. That room has now come to symbolise the cooperative spirit in which staff at the Crèche and the Kweekschool helped each other: the seed from which their subsequent efforts to save those children would grow. Working together they built up the mutual trust which was so essential when helping those going into hiding and for resistance in general. In this room the museum brings back the voices of witnesses: here it is the Jewish and non-Jewish rescuers who helped children escape from the Crèche. Their voices describe the complex logistics involved in helping children, the dilemmas and the risks. An animation on the wall visualises the rescue of children from the Crèche.

The various multimedia installations in the Kweekschool and the Hollandsche Schouwburg supply the historical narrative of the location. A thin line separates enabling visitors to get a sense of the history and reconstructing a historical situation. The National Holocaust Museum balances on that line to satisfy the curiosity of visitors anxious to know what the place looked like and how it functioned during the war. That sense of authenticity remains hugely important. It brings history closer, providing the tools to enable visitors to empathise. And that is crucial when attempting to tell the history of the Shoah. At the very place where it happened, visitors are given the most complete, nuanced picture of historical events. To do justice to the victims of the Shoah and at the same time to treat the distance in time and the distance from the suffering they endured with respect. Because we can never know what it was really like.

Education at the National Holocaust Museum

Learning about and learning from the Holocaust

Marc van Berkel & Julia Sarbo

A museum like the National Holocaust Museum is about far more than descriptions of the horrors of the persecution of Jews during the Second World War. Its mission is to encourage visitors to reflect about how that history impacts on our conduct in this day and age.

◁ **Before the Second World War, Jewish life in the Netherlands varied enormously. Objects and images of everyday life, Jewish tradition and leisure activities from the Netherlands and overseas territories illustrate that diversity.** Jewish Museum collection, photo by Thijs Wolzak.

The National Holocaust Museum has come about in response to the need to provide nuanced information about the history of the Shoah. Holocaust studies occupy a particular niche in the Dutch school syllabus. A visit to the National Holocaust Museum and the Hollandsche Schouwburg provides an important educational experience, broadening knowledge and evoking emotion, inviting visitors to reflect about their experiences. The educational interpretation of the museum's motto – seeing generates thought, thought generates action – encourages visitors to take an active stance.

So what is the museum trying to achieve? What do today's visitors, particularly young visitors, learn about the Holocaust? And in a society in which prejudice, discrimination, racism and antisemitism are once again rife, how important is Holocaust education? 'Ask yourself a question, and then ask someone else that same question.' This quote from Remco Campert is an attitude that we try to foster among the museum's school visitors. But how do we achieve that? How can we encourage young people's curiosity, and get them to ask questions and look for answers?

Here, at the National Holocaust Museum's historic location, visitors learn through personal stories about the history of the persecution of the Jews. Viewing the displays, they are introduced to Jewish life before the war and they discover that Jews formed an integral part of Dutch society. In rooms about the original purpose of the building visitors learn about childcare workers at the Crèche, the kindergarten opposite the Hollandsche Schouwburg, who saved the lives of hundreds of children. The presentation includes a page from a diary kept by a Jewish father, writing jokingly about an antisemitic remark his daughter heard from a friend.

Various sources bring visitors closer to people who lived through the Shoah, as if looking over their shoulder into the past. The aim is to spark curiosity and prompt visitors to engage with the historical context.

School visits start in one of our educational rooms where students have an opportunity to discuss the subject before their visit and then talk about what they have seen after. They are also encouraged to view the collection, to do their own research and to discover what happened here. Talking about choices and dilemmas in wartime challenges young people to reflect and to think about how the history of the persecution of the Jews impacts on today's world. This encounter with history encourages visitors to look at how these events relate to injustice in our own time: racism and antisemitism, war, violence and oppression. The museum's educational programmes are led by museum educators trained in guiding discussions that can become complex and challenging.

The reburial of Hannie Schaft and other resisters at Overveen honorary cemetery. This was when the burial ground was inaugurated, 27 November 1945. North Holland archive collection, 1478 -photos and negatives by Fotopersbureau De Boer in Haarlem, 321, photo by C. de Boer.

Holocaust education in Dutch schools

Every student in the Netherlands learns about the Second World War and the Holocaust at some point in the last two years of primary school. In high school, students learn about the topic in history lessons, although history isn't mandatory after the age of 15. That means that around 65 percent of Dutch students actually stop learning about history in later years at school.

Recent research has shown that interest in the Second World War and the Holocaust remains undiminished among both teachers and students. Teachers generally agree that the subject is important. Many young people learn about the Second World War and the Holocaust through school, literature or films and other visual media. Nevertheless, knowledge about the Holocaust is declining among students. One explanation is that our collective memory and representation of war and oppression in teaching materials tend to be formed by visual media such as films, documentaries and games. These interpretations are often superficial, lacking in nuance and sometimes historically incorrect. Meanwhile, as the years pass, fewer eyewitnesses remain to talk about the war from personal experience.

Teachers often find it hard to talk about the Holocaust in a responsible way with students. Some feel that their knowledge about the topic is inadequate, while some lack the necessary pedagogical tools. Students sometimes respond emotionally to the subject, especially if their own family was affected, or if they have experienced violence or conflict themselves. Some teachers become embroiled in fierce debates when they introduce the topic of the Holocaust, with those who link it to the situation in the Middle East. While the Holocaust is a compulsory subject in the history syllabus, the government has not issued any requirements regarding the way it should be taught. Teachers are largely free to tackle it as they see fit, as long as they follow the syllabus. Some teachers spend little time and have insufficient knowledge, others are well prepared and well informed. As a result, the quality of Holocaust education in the Netherlands varies enormously.

In the first years after the war, education about the Second World War in the Netherlands was mainly about encouraging the next generation to build a better future, focusing on freedom, truth, justice, solidarity, national unity and fraternity. The topic was linked to the Dutch population's resolute anti-fascism, to the courage and tenacity of an occupied nation: a story we now identify as the resistance myth. The Holocaust did not feature prominently in that narrative. Former Dutch resisters and successive Dutch governments refused to focus on Jews as a separate group. As a result, there was little public empathy for the experiences of persecuted Jews. The suffering of the population under Nazi occupation and the experiences of the resistance were considered to be far more important.

Generalisations were common in the school curriculum: Dutch fascists were considered a malign minority. Well into the 1970s, schools rarely taught about the persecution of Dutch Jews. The Holocaust was discussed in the context of national socialism and the Third Reich, as if the Dutch had nothing to do with the persecution. In the 1960s, new publications were signalling a change. Television

Dr Lou de Jong discusses the Nazi occupation in his television series *De Bezetting*. Spaarnestad Photo collection.

SS officer Adolf Eichmann standing trial in Israel, 1961. He was found guilty and executed. National Photo Collection of Israel.

Memorial for those deported from the Hollandsche Schouwburg. Jewish Museum collection.

programmes such as *De Bezetting* (The Occupation), and prosecutions of captured Nazis, such as the trial of Adolf Eichmann in Israel, brought the experience of victims of persecution and their children to public attention. A key development in the Jewish community in the Netherlands was the establishment of the Hollandsche Schouwburg as a *lieu de mémoire* in 1962: it was one of the first memorials dedicated specifically to the Jewish victims. With the reform of the Dutch education system (Mammoetwet), which came into force in 1968, Dutch schools began increasingly to view the persecution of Dutch Jewry as an important topic. New guidelines for history education were introduced, particularly the development of critical thinking skills. Gradually, the simplistic perception of the Holocaust as a Nazi campaign against Jews, made way for a more nuanced analysis of those tragic events which had happened in full view of the public and with the collaboration of many ellow citizens.

Fouten in de tv-serie over jodenvervolging

Van onze radio- en tv-redactie

ROTTERDAM – De spraakmakende televisieserie Holocaust zit op niet geheel onbelangrijke detailpunten vol historische fouten.

Ze brachten Peter Schulz-Kohr, dramachef van de Westduitse Süd-West-Funk ertoe om te zeggen: „Ze brengen de jeugd in verwarring en oudere Duitsers die de massale slachting nooit als gegeven hebben geaccepteerd zullen zeggen: zie je wel, dit klopt al niet eens, dan zal de rest ook wel onzin zijn".

Uniformen

In de 4-delige serie worden rangonderscheidingstekens onjuist gebruikt, uniformen kloppen soms niet. Hitlerjeugd zit in zomeruniformen onder de kerstboom en op het moment dat er al lang geen Pools leger meer bestaat treden er in de serie in een Pools getto soldaten op in Poolse uniformen. De opstand in het getto van Warschau begint volgens de serie op 8 mei 1943, terwijl de historische datum 18 april is.

Fouten

Ook prof. dr. L. de Jong, directeur van het rijksinstituut voor oorlogsdocumentatie, constateerde fouten. In Televizier van volgende week somt hij ze op: een joodse dokter heeft in 1935 nog een algemene kliniek, dat was toen al onmogelijk. De jodenster werd in 1941 ingevoerd; in Holocaust loopt men er al twee jaar eerder mee. Maar later in de serie lopen er joden zonder ster. In de kampen werd men kaal geschoren; in de serie hebben alle gevangenen haar. In de film controleert het Rode Kruis vaker dan in de werkelijkheid de kampen.

Hoewel in de oorlog elk fotootje werd afgepakt, laat de serie mensen in kampen zien die nog foto's in hun bezit hebben. Er zijn te gemakkelijke grenspassages, de kleding in de kampen is te mooi en men draagt echte schoenen in plaats van houten plankjes.

Prof. dr. De Jong constateert voorts ernstige atmosferische fouten. Er is geen moment te zien van honger, ontbering of werkelijke angst, terwijl dat de kenmerken zijn geweest van wat er met de joden is gebeurd.

Ondanks al die fouten is de serie inmiddels door ruim 20 landen gekocht. Naast België, Nederland en Duitsland zijn dat Engeland (vorige week uitgezonden), Turkije, Australië, Brazilië, Jamaica, Columbia, Guatemala, Hong Kong, Zuid-Korea, Tanzania, Filippijnen, Puerto Rico, Venezuela, Japan, Finland, Zweden, Panama, Canada en Thailand. Frankrijk twijfelt nog.

Verdeeldheid over Holocaust

• Prof. dr. L. de Jong: „Geen seconde ontroering".

Prof. dr. De Jong: Niet pijnlijk genoeg, film schiet tekort

Van onze radio- en tv-redactie

AMSTERDAM – Een krenking voor allen die de werkelijkheid van de jodenvervolging hebben meegemaakt. Zo karakteriseert prof. dr. J. P. van Praag de Amerikaanse televisieserie Holocaust in een brief aan besturen en directies van Tros en BRT.

Prof. dr. Van Praag is voorzitter van het werk- en adviescollege voor immateriële hulpverlening aan oorlogsgetroffenen (WAC). Deze organisatie twijfelt aan het nut van begeleiding door forumdiscussie, zoals BRT binnenkort en Tros begin volgend jaar in hun programma zullen opnemen. Bij eerdere gelegenheden is gebleken dat de verwarring door dergelijke discussies alleen maar groter wordt.

De secretaris van het WAC, dr. H. Leliefeld, noemde het aankoopbedrag van de serie – voor Nederland ongeveer 50.000 gulden – weggegooid geld. „Daarmee hadden enkele uitstekende voorlichtingsfilms gemaakt kunnen worden."

Over Holocaust is de mening in de joodse gemeenschap sterk verdeeld. Op verzoek van het blad Televizier bekeken een aantal gezaghebbende joden de 7 uur durende film. In het nummer van volgende week worden hun uitspraken en een uitgebreide discussie met BRT en Tros gepubliceerd.

Vrijwel iedereen had bedenkingen tegen de serie, maar over de vraag of zo'n niet geheel vlekkeloos gemaakt verhaal, waarin nogal wat romantiek voorkomt, wèl of niet moet worden uitgezonden liepen de antwoorden uiteen.

Voor en tegen

Vóór uitzending zijn: de arts J. Z. Baruch, rabbijn B. Drukarch van het Portugees-Israëlitisch kerkgenootschap, mevrouw H. C. van Meekren en S. Meijer van het centrum voor de joodse geestelijke gezondheidszorg, en prof. dr. L. de Jong, directeur van het rijksintituut voor oorlogsdocumentatie.

Tégen de serie zijn: drs. N. Boeken en mevrouw F. de Vries van het joods maatschappelijk werk, H. van den Elsen, maatschappelijk werker van de joodse geestelijke gezondheidszorg, opperrabbijn M. Just, dr. L. Leertouwer, docent rijksuniversiteit Groningen, en rabbijn J. Soetendorp van de liberaal joodse gemeente.

Baruch is voorstander omdat ondanks alle romances de kijker wordt geinformeerd over de gruwelen van de oorlog, zodat ook het ontstaan van Israël duidelijk wordt. Rabbijn Drukarch noemt in Televizier de serie een zwakke zaak, maar verwacht dat Holocaust met name bij jongeren begrip zal opwekken.

• Inga Weiss (Meryl Streep) wordt door een Duitse kampwacht weggeduwd nadat zij, dank zij de hulp van een verliefde nazi, haar man in Buchenwald heeft bezocht. Een door prof. dr. L. de Jong betwiste scène uit Holocaust, want bezoeken waren onmogelijk in die tijd.

Morgenavond:
Holocaust
21.05 uur
België Vlaams 1

Datzelfde geldt voor mevrouw Van Meekren en S. Meijer.

Tussen de voorstanders neemt dr. L. de Jong een aparte plaats in. „Deze serie heeft me geen seconde ontroerd. Ik vind dat ze tekort schiet. De NCRV heeft de serie afgewezen omdat Holocaust te pijnlijk is. Ik moet u zeggen: ik vind de serie niet pijnlijk genoeg. En dat is eigenlijk veel erger."

De Jong is vóór uitzending omdat de buurlanden België, Frankrijk en Engeland dat ook doen en veel mensen op die manier al kennis kunnen nemen van het verhaal.

De tegenstanders: opperrabbijn Just: „Er zit te veel kitsch in". Drs. N. Boeken vreest dat de serie vooral verkeerd overkomt bij degenen die al hulp nodig hebben. „Niet eens omdat ze bepaalde zaken herkennen, maar juist omdat ze heel veel dingen niet terug zien die zij juist als een verschrikkelijke ervaring hebben beleefd".

Boeken pleit voor meer voorlichting over de verschrikkingen die joden hebben meegemaakt. „Holocaust is daar helaas een ondeugdelijk middel voor".

Mevrouw F. de Vries: vindt het een slechte film en is erg teleurgesteld: „De joden worden door deze film heus niet zo gekwetst, want ze zijn al genoeg gekwetst". H. van den Elsen: „Deze vertekening doet geen recht aan de getroffenen".

Dr. L. Leertouwer: „Ik denk dat deze serie weinig effect zal hebben. Echt gedenken moet je van je ouders leren, dat kan niet via de televisie".

Rabbijn Soetendorp in Televizier: „Natuurlijk moet er informatie zijn, maar als die onzorgvuldig is worden er juist wonden open gereten. Zoals het in Holocaust gebeurt is het een trivialisering van de werkelijkheid. Als je feiten en fantasie vermengt, en zeker bij dit probleem, loop je het gevaar dat mensen gaan zeggen: wat is nu waar en wat niet?"

Het Nieuw Israëlitisch Weekblad reageert deze week ook op Holocaust. In een hoofdartikel kondigt dit blad „Een felle discussie met golven van emotie" aan. Het blad zegt ook: „Holocaust is een verschrikkelijke film. Een film die pijn zal doen".

Het enige joodse opinieweekblad van ons land is desondanks voorstander van uitzending: „Want Holocaust heeft veel te zeggen. De boodschap die hij heeft te brengen is in het belang van de vervolgden en hun kinderen. Ondanks de pijn die hij aan de vervolgden zal doen. Dezen zouden zelfbeheersing moeten betrachten door het tv-scherm blind te laten in de tijd van uitzending (....) Hoe erg de film ook zal overkomen, de werkelijkheid was vreselijker".

Juist omdat de serie zachter is dan de werkelijkheid noemt het NIW uitzending acceptabel. „Een film met alleen de harde werkelijkheid, zonder romantisering, zonder commercialisering zou in opzet zijn mislukt. Hij zou niet zijn aan te zien. Geen uur".

◁ **Review of *Holocaust* television series in *Algemeen Dagblad* newspaper, September 1978.** DPG Media Group collection.

The broadcast of American television series *Holocaust* in the Netherlands in 1979 stimulated new initiatives in Holocaust education. This series about a fictional Jewish family was the first television programme in the Netherlands to show the Holocaust from the perspective of the victims. Educators produced information brochures and teaching materials, sketching didactic and educational approaches in which euphemisms in Nazi terminology were explained in clear, contemporary idiom, alongside survivors' testimonies. The resistance myth also came under fire: many people had stood by passively as the persecution took place, some Dutch citizens had been actively involved. In the Netherlands, antisemitism had existed before the war; many people had been largely uninterested in the fate of the Jews. The vision of collective heroism in the face of the enemy, made way for another narrative: that of the culpable bystander.

Educational value of an authentic site: 'It happened here'

Holocaust education has changed considerably in the Netherlands in recent years. Research indicates that it has become increasingly individualised and linked to emotions, particularly due to the many personal testimonies that are available online. In the 1990s, people who had lived through the war were regularly invited to speak at schools: these guest appearances were arranged by various organisations. Later, Holocaust education came to be associated with other human rights issues and the Holocaust became a universal symbol in the campaign against discrimination, racism and antisemitism. At the same time, educators placed more emphasis on local and regional aspects of the Holocaust. Throughout the Netherlands, dozens of local *lieux de mémoires* were identified: memorial sites established by tourism professionals, heritage preservers, survivors and their family and friends.

The historic legacy of the National Holocaust Museum and the Hollandsche Schouwburg as authentic locations contributes greatly to their educational value: it was from here that people were deported. At least some were rescued.

As the number of those who witnessed what happened declines, the educational importance of this historic location becomes all the more powerful. Research shows that many teachers and students believe that the authenticity of a historical site makes it particularly interesting and special. Teachers are not always aiming to instil knowledge about the history of the Second World War and the Holocaust on school visits to museums and sites. They will often have dealt with the historical context in class beforehand. Research carried out in 2021, shows that eighty percent of teachers chose to visit memorial centres and war museums because these were authentic sites. Or, as one teacher responded: 'To literally touch the past.' He elucidated: 'Not all the students are interested in history, and sensitivity among young people towards this topic is declining.' Teachers and students often visit authentic locations offering historical information, personal perspectives and background as part of a historical experience. Researchers refer to this as the rediscovery of *lieux de mémoires* as authentic sites.

Memorial at Westerbork concentration camp containing 102,000 stones, unveiled in 1992. HCKW collection, photo by Sake Elzinga.

Salo Muller talking about his experiences at the Hollandsche Schouwburg and the Crèche. Jewish Museum collection, photo by Nienke Fonk.

Different levels of experience

In Dutch schools, learning about the Holocaust has largely made way for learning from the Holocaust. What we can learn from the Holocaust, and the Second World War in general, has been the topic of much discussion, here and abroad. British historian David Cesarani has criticised the way an unhistorical Holocaust has been instrumentalised in schools, leading students to disregard historical accuracy. He argued that to be able to learn from history we must first learn about history. Canadian historian Michael Marrus put it another way: 'My principal lesson of the Holocaust is, therefore, beware of lessons.'

The National Holocaust Museum's goal is to increase the desire to learn more about this topic, to encourage visiting students to do research and to pose questions. In practice, schools teach about the Holocaust as part of the Second World War. Auschwitz has become the central theme in Holocaust education, and for many students this is their only association with the topic. But because the killing of six million Jews did not begin or end at Auschwitz, the museum is more specifically concerned with events preceding the camps, such as the vilification of Jewish stereotypes, the discrimination, segregation and dispossession of property that took place across the Netherlands. To illustrate this, the presentation shows Nazi regulations which Dutch bureaucrats were required to implement. These anti-Jewish orders affected every aspect of public and personal life.

In line with the museum's goal to promote education, questions are posted at various points in the presentation to encourage visitors to reflect. Digital installations and audio recordings in which experts talk about historically relevant events. One of the installations in the presentation is about the impact anti-Jewish regulations had on everyday life. Visitors learn about the effects of discrimination and about the options people had at the time. Another installation shows how the Nazis used propaganda and misinformation. The film that the Nazis ordered to be made at Westerbork transit camp is a central exhibit in the presentation.

At Klem 9/12, visitors read diary extracts written by Westerbork camp prisoners. The quotes contrast starkly with the film clips shown.
Jewish Museum collection, photo by Thijs Wolzak.

The installation shows how information can be used to mislead people. It encourages a more critical approach to research and to other available sources. A third installation examines how war criminals were tried after the war. In an audio recording, an expert describes how the Nazis dismantled the legal certainties on which Dutch society is founded and the importance of a functioning democratic system.

The last display shows Jewish life in the postwar period with testimonies by survivors and later generations describing how the Holocaust impacts on their life. These are the children and grandchildren of survivors and victims. The interviews give a sense of the ongoing effect of discrimination, prejudice and hate, and of the murder of family members. Yet they also reflect the resilience of the Jewish community and the ability of Jewish families to recover and grow.

Connecting with the present

In addition to experiencing the museum as an authentic location and a place to learn, the museum also helps teachers and students link the history of the persecution of Jews in the Netherlands to contemporary issues. Young people want to know how war, prejudice, discrimination and racism relate to the Holocaust. They want to be able to make connections and comparisons. A large majority of Dutch teachers feel that young people are able to learn lessons from the history of the Holocaust. In their studies, they link the historical context of the Holocaust to contemporary moral problems. This relates to the moral dimension discussed in civics lessons: the study of history can stimulate the development of moral and democratic values through comparisons between past and present, and the encouragement of critical thinking about principles, norms and values. Historical insight can improve our understanding of the present day.

The Second World War and the Holocaust took place amid a crisis of democracy, a failure of the rule of law, antisemitism, racism, discrimination and much besides. Yet historical reality is complex, and this complexity may be difficult to convey in an educational or didactic context. The National Holocaust Museum collection has many different objects relating to stories which teachers can use to connect in meaningful ways with the past and the present.

The museum's educational programme begins by examining what happened at the Crèche and the Hollandsche Schouwburg. Students learn about people, objects and events that relate in significant ways to the history of the Holocaust. Knowledge about that history is crucial for a better understanding of the circumstances in which the events of that time took place. In effect, students learn about the Holocaust in order to be able to draw lessons for the present.

In an installation about anti-Jewish regulations, visitors discover the impact of each additional exclusion. Jewish Museum collection, photo by Thijs Wolzak.

Students learn about the Holocaust by observing, listening and researching. They work in groups and assess the collection together. They engage in discussions about what these past events mean today. Visiting the National Holocaust Museum helps young people develop a personal connection with the Shoah. It offers them a chance to reflect and form an opinion. A key aspect of Holocaust education is learning to identify the language of the perpetrators, the propaganda and antisemitism before, during and after the war, and to understand what happens when democratic values and the basic legal certainties are undermined. Holocaust education is also about acquiring skills such as insight and the ability to interpret historical sources and testimony. The overall goal of knowledge and expertise is to be able to connect with the past and the present. Ultimately, our aim is to combat indifference: show you care, make a difference.

homes. **29-05-1942**: Jews may no longer go fishing. **01-06-1942**: the *Bureau Joodsche Zaken*, an office of Jewish affairs, is set up within the Amsterdam police department. This bureau is responsible for everything related to violations of anti-Jewish regulations. **01-06-1942**: a total of 173 Jewish men from The Hague are sent to a labour camp in the province of Friesland. **05-06-1942**: Jews may no longer travel. Exceptions are possible for urgent matters, such as illness, death, funerals or exams. **11-06-1942**: the number of Jews to be deported from France, Belgium and the Netherlands is decided upon in Berlin. By the end of the year, the first 15,000 Jews must be deported from the Netherlands to Auschwitz. **11-06-1942**: Jews are no longer allowed to shop at fish markets. **12-06-1942**: Jews may only buy vegetables from Jewish shopkeepers or at outdoor markets designated for Jews. **12-06-1942**: all Jews must turn in their bicycles. **12-06-1942**: any form of sport in public is forbidden for Jews. This includes rowing, canoeing, swimming, playing tennis or football. **16-06-1942**: the belongings of deported Jews are to be confiscated. These household goods will be sent to occupied areas in Eastern Europe. Most, however, will end up in German cities ravaged by bombings. **18-06-1942**: the number of Jewish men in labour camps located in the Netherlands must be increased to 4,500 before 15 July. **19-06-1942**: Jewish doctors performing health checks are replaced by NSB doctors. From now on, almost every Jew is approved to be sent to a labour camp. **20-06-1942**: more and more professions are forbidden for Jews. Especially in the financial and economic sector. Also, Jews with occupations such as gymnastic instructors, massage therapists, beauticians and barbers may only have Jewish clients. **22-06-1942**: the previously determined number of 15,000 Jews to be deported is adjusted. By the year's end, 40,000 Jews must be deported from the Netherlands to Auschwitz. **25-06-1942**: in the province of Groningen, all Jewish men between the ages of 16 and 55 must receive health checks and be approved for deployment to labour camps. **25-06-1942**: in the provinces of Friesland and Drenthe, all Jewish men between the ages of 18 and 58 must also be approved for deployment to labour camps. **26-06-1942**: an announcement that Jews between the ages of 16 and 40, women as well as men, will be sent to Germany to be 'employed in work camps'. In reality, these are deportations to Auschwitz. The Westerbork refugee camp will be used as a transit camp. **29-06-1942**: the German Commissioner-General responsible for special affairs states in a speech that Jews 'will return there as poorly from whence they came'. This is then published in the Dutch newspapers about the upcoming deportations. **30-06-1942**: the German authorities demand that 600 Jews per day are sent to Germany to be 'employed in work camps'. The age limit is set at 40. The occupier promises that families will not be separated and corresponding by mail will be possible. Employees of the Jewish Council are exempt from deportation for the time being. **30-06-1942**: Jews must stay indoors between 8 pm and 6 am. During these hours Jews may not be in the homes of non-Jews. **30-06-1942**: Jews may only visit non-Jewish shops between 3 pm and 5 pm. **30-06-1942**: Jews are no longer allowed to work as street peddlers. **30-06-1942**: Jews are banned from using public transport. There are exceptions. A permit must be obtained from the Sicherheitspolizei, German security police. Jews are only allowed to travel third class. Jews may only be seated once all non-Jews have a place to sit. **30-06-1942**: Jews may no longer use public telephones. **01-07-1942**: Westerbork, in the east of the Netherlands, is now a transit camp under German police supervision. Erich Deppner is appointed the Commandant of the camp. **03-07-1942**: more details about restrictions enacted on 30 June are published in *Het Joodsche Weekblad*: Jews must stay at home between 8 pm and 6 am. Only Jews with travel permits may be at an address other than their own at night. The 8 pm to 6 am curfew does not apply to Jewish doctors and midwives with a special night permit. **04-07-1942**: thousands of notices for 'employment' in Germany are dispatched. Especially German and other non-Dutch Jews will receive these call-ups. The youngest of them are 16 years old. The notices are delivered on Sunday 5 July. In the days that follow, another 3,000 call-up notices go out. **06-07-1942**: Jews may no longer visit any non-Jews at home. **06-07-1942**: Jews are no longer allowed to have telephones. **09-07-1942**: service for tram line 8 in Amsterdam is terminated. The route goes right through the Jewish quarter. Since Jews have been banned from using public transport, line 8 has only very few passengers. **10-07-1942**: around 850 Jewish men from Groningen are sent to different labour camps in the provinces Drenthe and Overijssel. Some of them are transported to Westerbork. **10-07-1942**: Jews are no longer permitted to lean out their windows, be on their balconies or in gardens facing the street. In front of open windows, the yellow star must be visible on their clothing. **12-07-1942**: Call-up notices for 'employment' are now delivered by Amsterdam police officers. Recipients of these call-ups must report the next day to the *Zentralstelle*. **14-07-1942**: the German authorities want to prevent the text of a protest telegram against the upcoming deportations from being read aloud in churches. They ease regulations for Jews who have converted to Christianity and those in mixed marriages. **14-07-1942**: in the centre of Amsterdam, the German police arrest 540 Jewish men and women. They are held hostage to be deported if the 4,000 Jews who received call-ups do not report as ordered. **14-07-1942**: at 2:16 am, the first train from Amsterdam Central Station departs for Hooghalen Station nearby Westerbork transit camp. Aboard are 962 Jewish men, women and children who complied with the call-up notices. **15-07-1942**: the first deportation train leaves Westerbork. Aboard are 1,135 Jewish men, women and children. Their final destination is Auschwitz concentration and extermination camp. **15-07-1942**: the German authorities order the Dutch Railways to build a direct train line from Hooghalen Station to Camp Westerbork. **16-07-1942**: the first deportation train from Camp Amersfoort leaves for Westerbork. From there 309 men are deported to Auschwitz. **17-07-1942**: the first deportation train from the Netherlands arrives at Auschwitz. Many of those aboard are gassed shortly after their arrival. **17-07-1942**: in The Hague, a number of streets and squares are declared off-limits to Jews. **20-07-1942**: Amsterdam's *Hollandsche Schouwburg* – the former Dutch Theatre – is turned into a deportation centre for Jews who have been detained. Here they must await their deportation to Westerbork. **30-07-1942**: about 1,100 Jews from Rotterdam are deported to Westerbork from Loods 24, a warehouse used as a deportation centre. **31-07-1942**: Jews may no longer visit hairdressing salons owned by non-Jews. **01-08-1942**: anyone with a telephone must fill in an Aryan declaration. Jews and those who refuse will have their telephone service disconnected. **02-08-1942**: a *razzia* against Jews who have converted to Catholicism. This is a reprisal for the protest against the persecution of Jews read aloud in Catholic churches on 26 July. Some Dutch Reformed Churches also read out the text, but Jews who have become Protestant suffer no consequences. **06-08-1942**: in Amsterdam, 1,600 Jews are arbitrarily rounded up in the streets or removed from their homes and detained as hostages. This is to pressure Jews who received call-ups to report. There are threats to send these Jewish hostages to Mauthausen. **07-08-1942**: Jews who do not obey the call-up notices are also threatened with deportation to Mauthausen. This applies as well to Jews who refuse to wear the yellow star, those who wear it incorrectly and people who have gone into hiding. The Jewish Council must announce this in *Het Joodsche Weekblad*. **09-08-1942**: *razzias* are also used to round up and deport Jews. In the south of Amsterdam, 270 Jews are arrested in such a raid and 230 of them are deported to Westerbork. **13-08-1942**: Switzerland closes its borders to Jews and others who 'for reasons of race' want to flee to that country. In the year that follows, 2,700 refugees will be sent back to Nazi-occupied Europe, including Jews from the Netherlands. **14-08-1942**: Jews may only enter government buildings in The Hague after an official request from German or Dutch authorities. **18-08-1942**: Jews from more and more cities are faced with deportation. Around 1,200 Jews from The Hague are deported to Westerbork. Included among them are war invalids from a military hospital and prisoners from the house of detention in nearby Scheveningen. **18-08-1942**: several hundred Jewish residents from the city of Utrecht must report for deportation to Westerbork. **18-08-1942**: all of Amersfoort's Jews between the ages of 16 and 40 must go to Westerbork. The remaining Jews in the city must relocate to Amsterdam within three days. **18-08-1942**: streets in Amsterdam named after Jews are given new, non-Jewish names. This also happens at different times in other places in the

Objects

Gerben Post

Twin cradle

Jewish Museum collection

From the autumn of 1942, the Crèche across the street from the Hollandsche Schouwburg housed children up to age thirteen. Separated from their parents who were detained in the theatre, the children awaited deportation there. This arrangement led Henriëtte Pimentel, the director of the Crèche, and Walter Süskind, who supervised the theatre's Jewish employees, to come up with the idea of smuggling children from the Crèche to safe hiding places. This could only be done once their parents had granted permission.

The non-Jewish friends Hester van Lennep and Pauline van Waasdijk, who ran a skincare institute, got involved in this 'children's work'. As part of the *Trouw* resistance group – one of the four organised groups involved – they risked their own lives to to temporarily shelter children above their salon on Keizersgracht. Later, the children were moved to other locations to go into hiding.

In the attic of the building, Hester and Pauline had as many as thirteen cradles for the youngest in hiding, including this twin cradle. It came from Hester's parents' home. She had slept in it herself as a baby. Hester and Pauline contributed to the rescue of more than six-hundred children.

Photograph

LIFE Picture Collection

Of the 140,000 Jews living in the Netherlands in May 1940, over 107,000 were deported to various concentration and extermination camps during five years of German occupation. One of the approximately 5,000 Dutch survivors of the camps was seven-year-old Sieg Maandag.

In February 1944, Sieg was deported along with his parents and sister from Westerbork to the German concentration camp Bergen-Belsen. When this camp was liberated on 15 April 1945, Sieg and his sister were barely alive. They also did not know the whereabouts of their parents. Sieg was photographed walking past a long row of dead bodies shortly after the liberation of Bergen-Belsen. In May 1945, this picture appeared in the American magazine *Life,* although in an edited version. Naked bodies were clothed and faces were rendered unrecognisable. An uncle in New York recognised Sieg and sent several copies to Sieg's mother in Amsterdam. Consequently, she discovered her son was still alive. Sieg and his sister were reunited with their mother. Their father did not survive the horrors of the camps.

Later in life, Sieg became a visual artist. His wartime experiences had a a lasting impact on him. Whenever he painted a self-portrait, Sieg always depicted two faces, with one invariably turned away.

Wedding dress

Jewish Museum collection
photo by Thijs Wolzak

On 12 March 1940, Grietje Sondervan helped her daughter Leny into this wedding gown. Grietje made this white dress from luxurious silk-satin with her own hands. That day, Leny married Frits Snapper, a reserve officer in the Dutch Army.

Frits wore his dress uniform on his wedding day. His accompanying sword was not allowed into the synagogue by the rabbi. For the wedding photo, Frits posed with an empty scabbard. His parents, brother and sister did not attend the wedding. Due to the increasing threat posed by Nazi Germany, they had already left the Netherlands. Leny's parents Jacob and Grietje were present in the synagogue for the *chuppah*, a reference to the Jewish wedding ceremony here.

During the war, Frits fled to Switzerland. There, he decided to cross the border into Italy to join the resistance. Leny joined the resistance in the Netherlands but was arrested and deported to Bergen-Belsen. Both survived the war. Jacob and Grietje Sondervan did not survive. They were murdered in Auschwitz on 18 November 1943.

Torch holder

Collection Stiftung Deutsches Historisches Museum, Berlin

Seven years before the 1940 German invasion and occupation of the Netherlands, Adolf Hitler became Reich Chancellor of Germany. Although his National Socialist Workers' Party (NSDAP) had been democratically elected, it did not take long for Germany to become a dictatorship. Hitler was a charismatic figure. After Germany's crushing defeat in the First World War, his vision was extremely appealing to many Germans. Hitler articulated precisely what people wanted to hear and promised to restore the country's honour. Using terror, intimidation and violence, the National Socialists gained the support of the populace. With compelling propaganda, uniforms, flags, a unique salute and symbolism, the Nazis awakened the nationalism of many Germans.

A good example of this is the torchlight procession that takes place during the Olympics. In the run-up to the 1936 Olympic Games in Berlin, this relay with the Olympic flame was introduced. More than 3,400 runners carried the torch from the ancient site of Olympia in Greece to Berlin. There, the flame was ceremoniously welcomed by 20,000 members of the Hitler Youth and 40,000 members of the Sturmabteilung, a security service of the NSDAP.

Craniometer

Collection Stichting Nationaal Museum van Wereldculturen

Nazi terror against political opponents and Jews began shortly after Hitler's rise to power. As early as April 1933, the Nazis proclaimed a boycott of Jewish-owned businesses and the Nuremberg Laws were enacted two years later. These laws determined who was considered Jewish and prohibited Jews from having (sexual) relationships with non-Jews. The same laws also applied to other groups deemed inferior by the Nazis such as Roma and Sinti.

National Socialist racist ideology was not a new concept. As early as the nineteenth century, the external features of groups of people were linked to behaviour and character traits.

Well into the twentieth century, scientists examined the facial features, hair growth, skin and eye colour of different groups of people. Their skulls were also measured, using a craniometer like this one.

These pseudoscientific ideas about race found supporters among fascists all across Europe. In Germany, the Nazis utilised assumed research findings to perfect the so-called 'Aryan race'. They denied the reality that there is, in fact, only one human race.

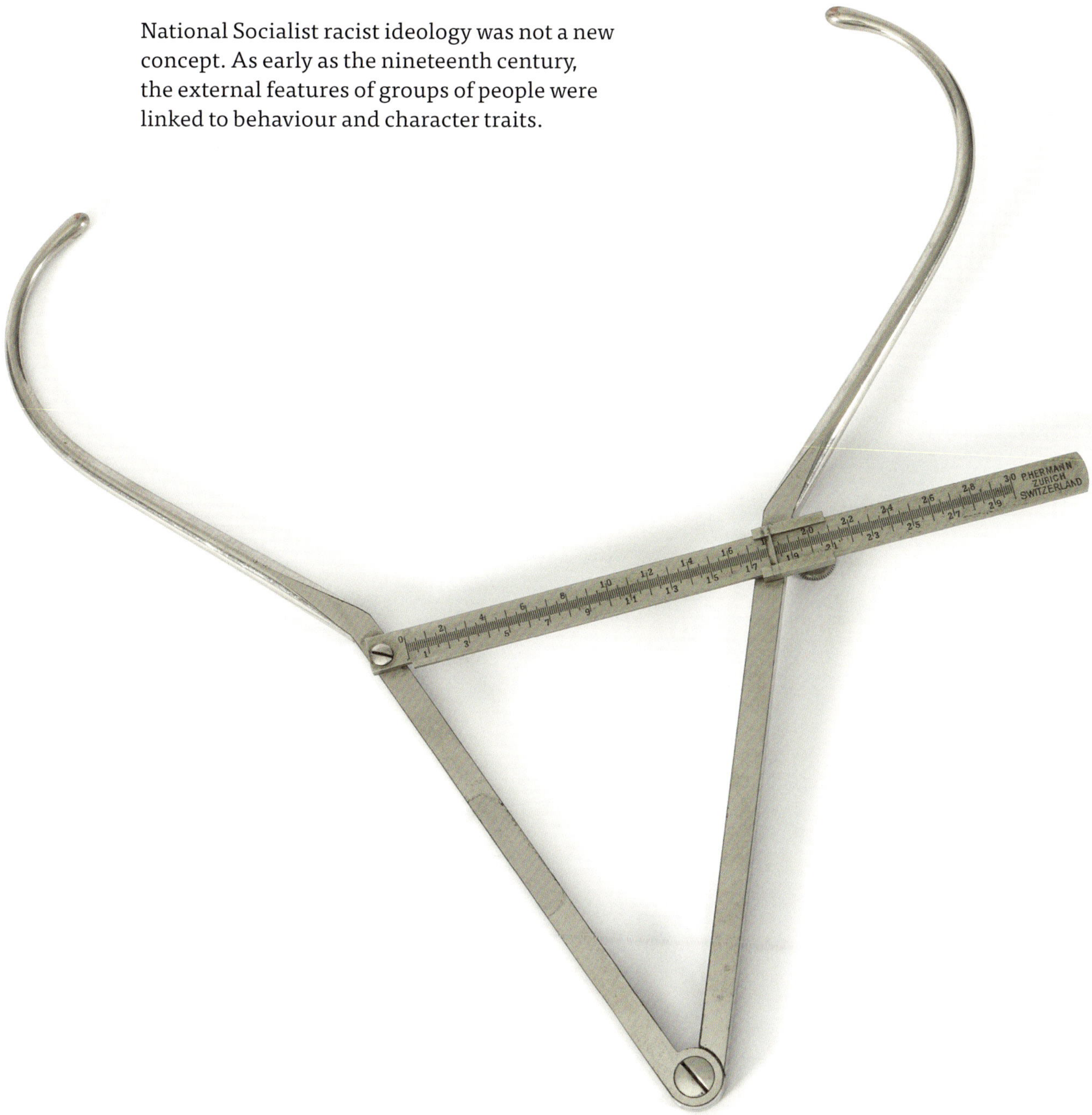

Prayer shawl

Jewish Museum collection

Walter and Johanna Süskind fled from Germany to the Netherlands in early 1938. Unlike many other asylum seekers, it was not difficult for them to stay n the country. In fact, Walter had two Dutch grandparents and therefore the Dutch nationality. As a result, they were also allowed to take some of their possessions with them. This *tallit*, a prayer shawl, most likely belonged to Walter.

Walter and Johanna settled in the city of Bergen op Zoom, where in 1939 their daughter Yvonne was born. During the occupation, the family was forcibly relocated to Amsterdam. There, Walter eventually became manager of the Hollandsche Schouwburg. Together with his employee Felix Halverstad and several other Jewish Council employees, Süskind played a pivotal role in orchestrating escapes from the theatre. He was also involved in rescuing over six-hundred children from the Crèche across the street.

The Süskind family was rounded up on 29 September 1943 and sent to Westerbork. Almost a year later, they were deported via Theresienstadt to Auschwitz, where Johanna and Yvonne were murdered immediately upon arrival. Walter himself was killed in January or February 1945, somewhere in Central Europe, during a death march to another camp.

Regulation books

Jewish Museum collection

On May 29, 1940, the Austrian jurist Arthur Seyss-Inquart was installed as Reich Commissioner of the Netherlands under occupation. He ecame the highest-ranking Nazi authority in the country. This took place in the *Ridderzaal* of the *Binnenhof* – the ceremonial hall at the seat of the Dutch parliament in The Hague. Numerous German military figures and both German and Dutch officials were in attendance.

Under Seyss-Inquart's administration, democracy was abolished and the Dutch parliament was dissolved. The rule of law was dismantled and replaced. The Dutch Supreme Court, the most important judicial body in the Netherlands, refused to test German ordinances against the *Landoorlogreglement* (Land War Regulations). This gave these ordinances, including the anti-Jewish measures, the appearance of legitimacy.

From 1941, more and more anti-Jewish measures were declared. These were announced and implemented by the Jewish Council. All these German ordinances were officially laid down in a so-called *Verordeningen Blad*, regulations leaflet. Each year of the occupation also saw the publication of these regulation books, in which all the leaflets of a respective year were collected into a single volume.

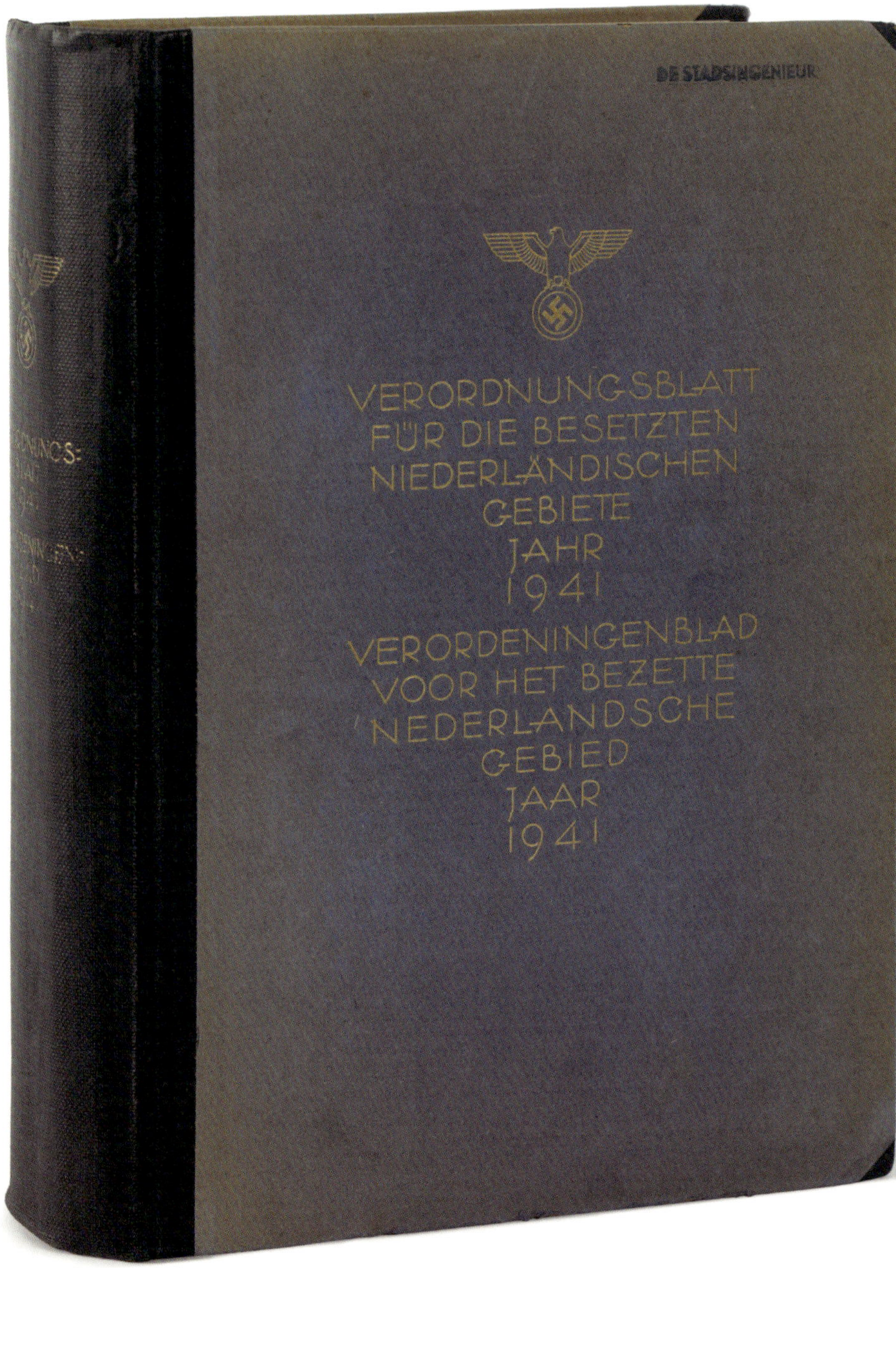

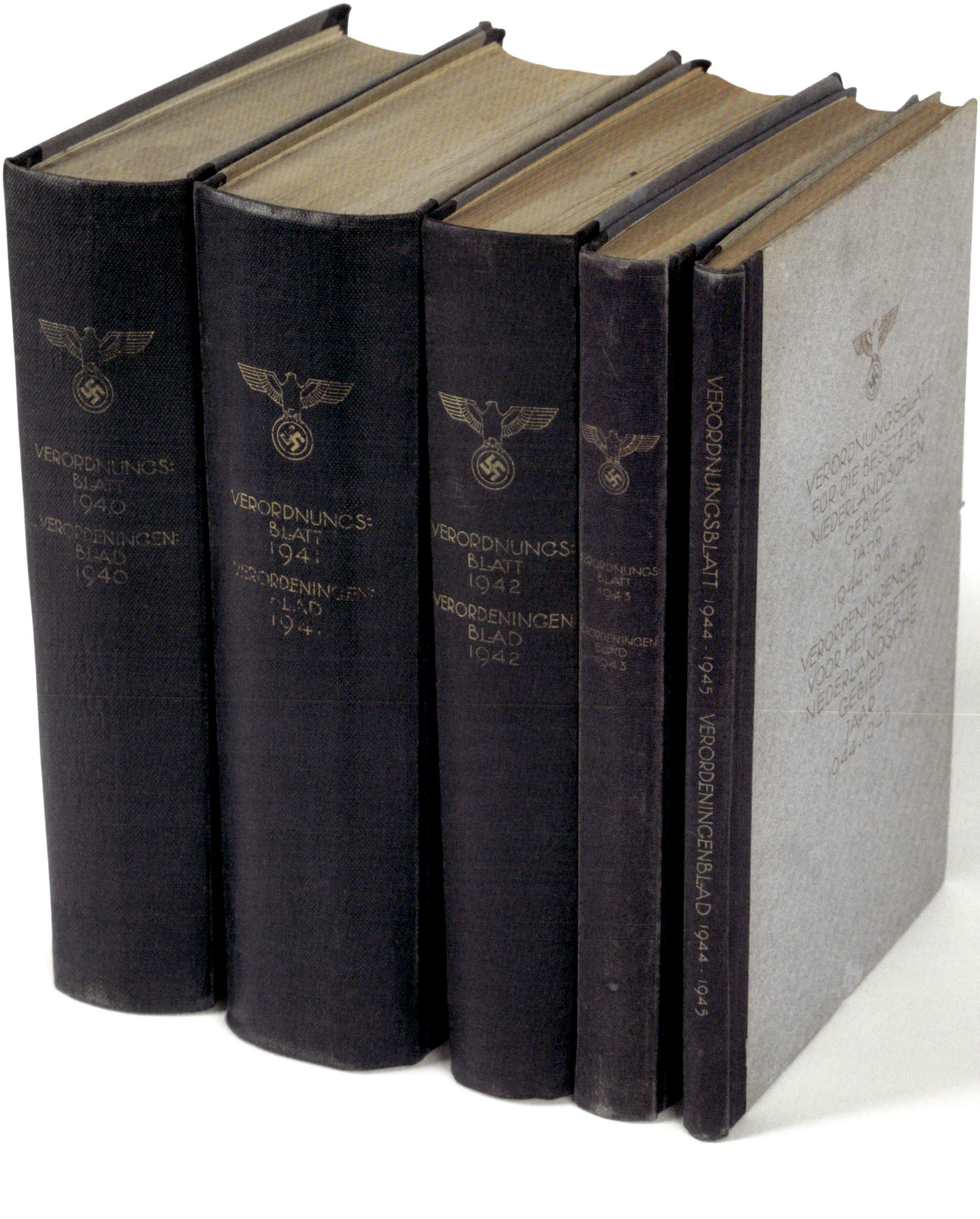
VERORDNUNGS-
BLATT
1940
VERORDENINGEN-
BLAD
1940
VERORDNUNGS-
BLATT
1941
VERORDENINGEN-
BLAD
1941
VERORDNUNGS-
BLATT
1942
VERORDENINGEN-
BLAD
1942
VERORDNUNGS-
BLATT
1943
VERORDENINGEN
BLAD
1943
VERORDNUNGSBLATT 1944 - 1945 VERORDENINGENBLAD 1944 - 1945
VERORDNUNGSBLATT
FÜR DIE BESETZTEN
NIEDERLÄNDISCHEN
GEBIETE
JAHR
1944-1945
VERORDENINGENBLAD
VOOR HET BEZETTE
NEDERLANDSCHE
GEBIED
JAAR
1944-1945

Card catalogue

Jewish Museum collection

By order of the German authorities, the Jewish Council for Amsterdam was established on 12 February 1941. This council would act as something of a Jewish 'state within a state'. After all, the Jewish community was subject to different rules and regulations than the rest of the Dutch population. Two prominent Jewish men were appointed to co-chair the Jewish Council: Professor of Ancient History David Cohen and diamond trader Abraham Asscher.

The Jewish Council was initially a service organisation focused on providing social support, education, healthcare and culture. Amsterdam was not unique in this regard. In 1941, there were approximately sixty local Jewish Councils active throughout the Netherlands. From the autumn of that year, these councils came under the umbrella of Amsterdam's Jewish Council, which was supposedly established as 'Jewish self-governance.' In reality, this council was used to carry out the persecution and deportation of their own people. Important instruments in this process were communication and registration.

By 10 January 1941, all the Jews in the Netherlands had already been required to register in the municipality where they lived. In the autumn of that same year, the Jewish Council was instructed to create its own registration of all the Jews living in the country. This involved recording personal information, family makeup, and general impressions about individuals on index cards. The cards were stored in these boxes.

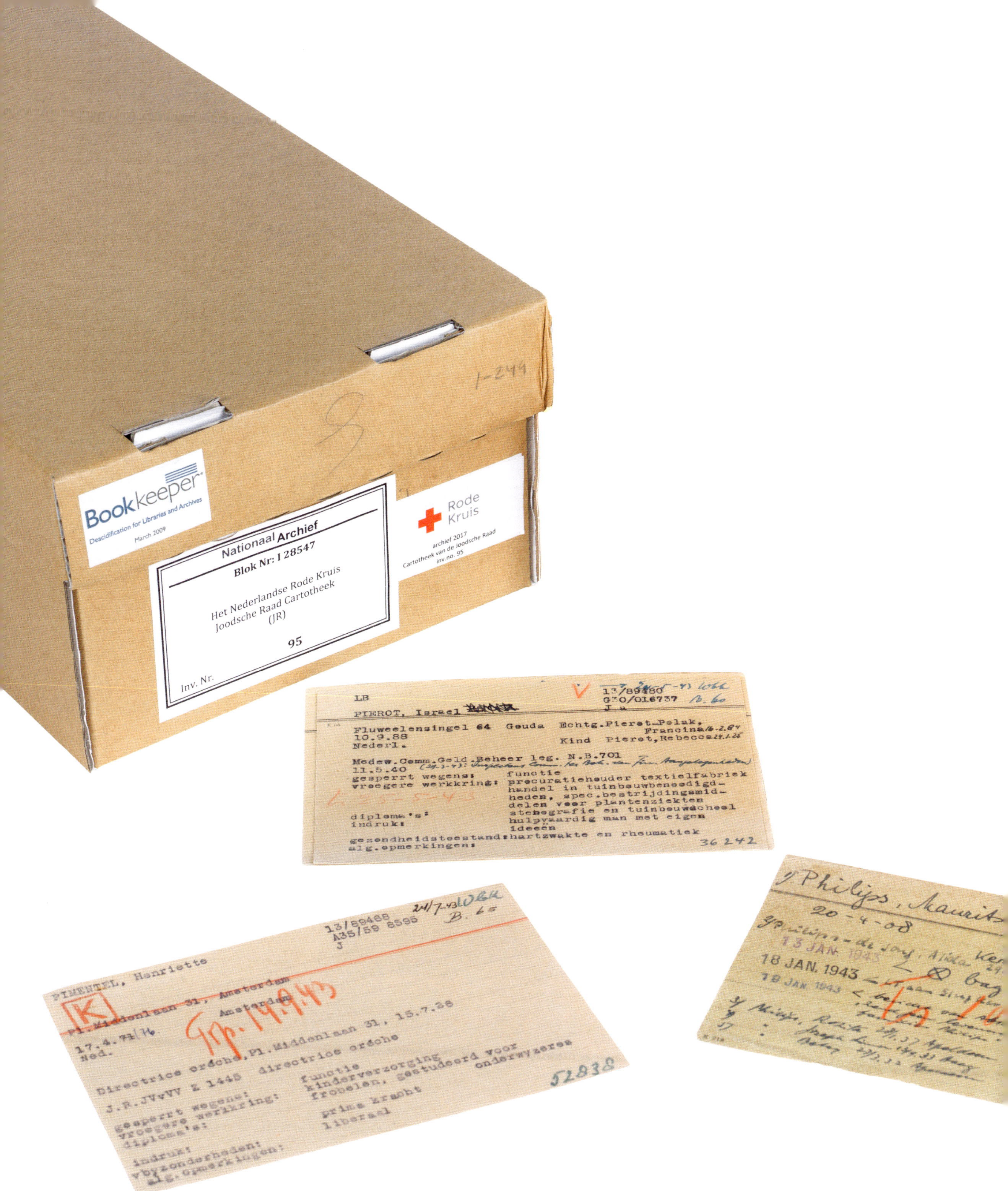

Bookkeeper
Deacidification for Libraries and Archives
March 2009
Nationaal Archief
Blok Nr: I 28547
Het Nederlandse Rode Kruis
Joodsche Raad Cartotheek
(JR)
95
Inv. Nr.
Rode Kruis
archief 2017
Cartotheek van de Joodsche Raad
inv.no. 95
PIEROT, Israel
Fluweelensingel 64 Gouda
gezondheidstoestand: hartzwakte en rheumatiek
PIMENTEL, Henriette
18 JAN. 1943

Barrack door

Jewish Museum collection

During the German occupation of the Netherlands, it was made increasingly difficult for Jews to practice their professions. For instance, Jews were only allowed to offer their services to other Jews. With this, the occupier wanted to ensure there would be little or no contact between Jews and non-Jews. As a result, part of the Jewish community fell into poverty, further increasing the distance between Jews and non-Jews.

On 10 October 1941, the German occupation authority decided to establish separate work camps for unemployed Jews in three northern provinces of the Netherlands. Administrative offices overseen by Amsterdam's mayor and city councillors and the Bureau Sociale Zaken – responsible for social services and welfare – assisted in identifying these Jewish men. Three months later, the Jewish Council was ordered to summon 1,400 out-of-work Jews to undergo health checks for employment. The first group of 905 men left for a work camp in the province of Drenthe on 10 January 1942. In the subsequent months, many more would follow.

From June 1942, 225 Jewish men, mostly from The Hague, were put to work in the Jewish labour camp Ybenheer, near the Frisian town of Fochteloo. There, they were forced to cut peat in the nearby wetlands. The men spent their evenings and nights in the camp in wooden barracks. This door is what remains of one of those shelters.

'Juda Verrek'

Jewish Museum collection

'Tears were running down my cheeks. He tried to console me, telling me things wouldn't get so bad.' On 15 May 1940, the day the Netherlands surrendered to Germany, the Jewish civil servant Meijer Lisser described in his diary a conversation he had with his non-Jewish manager. 'Here in the Netherlands, hardly anyone's an anti-semite,' and he continued, 'on the contrary.'

Once the occupation of the Netherlands became a reality, people had to adapt to an entirely new situation. This applied to Jews as well as non-Jews living in the county. A majority of the Dutch population tried as best as they could to carry on with their 'everyday lives', though a small percentage soon joined the resistance. Others actively turned against their Jewish neighbours.

The German occupation brought the latent anti-semitism of many Dutch people to the surface. Some even went as far as anticipating the implementation of anti-Jewish regulations by putting up signs stating Jews were no longer welcome. One of them was an anonymous Dutch man who wrote *Nederland ontwaak, Juda verrek* on this wooden board – 'Netherlands arise, Judah be damned.'

Yellow star

Jewish Museum collection

On 29 April 1942, the co-chairs of the Jewish Council were summoned to the German occupation authority. There they were informed of a new anti-Jewish measure that had to be announced the same day in *Het Joodsche Weekblad*, a Jewish weekly bulletin. It was one of the most humiliating measures up until that point.

From 3 May, every Jew aged six and older had to visibly wear a sewn-on patch in public places. It was a six-pointed Jewish star with the word 'Jew' printed in the centre in quasi-Hebrew letters. People had to pay for these yellow stars themselves. A month after a similar star had become compulsory in Germany in September 1941, the deportations of Germany's Jews began. The introduction of this star in the Netherlands therefore caused great anxiety.

A yellow star was also sewn on to this dress that once belonged to Amsterdam's Betty Appelboom. She was murdered in Sobibor on 7 May 1943, along with her parents and brother Dorus. Betty was thirteen years old.

B.APPELB.
Jood

Portrait of Albert van Raalte by Martin Monnickendam

Jewish Museum collection, donation art gallery Lilian

On 6 February 1942, the so-called *Steunactie* was established. The aim of this support initiative was to provide Jewish visual artists the opportunity to show and sell their work. For this purpose, an exhibition would be mounted in the Hollandsche Schouwburg – by that time called the Joodsche Schouwburg. Each Jewish artist could submit three artworks and the Van Leer Foundation would purchase one of them. The foundation also commissioned the renowned painter Martin Monnickendam to create a portrait of Albert van Raalte, the conductor of the Jewish Symphony Orchestra and former leader of the AVRO Orchestra, a popular radio ensemble.

In May 1941, orchestras were required to dismiss Jewish musicians. Shortly thereafter, some of them found new positions in the Jewish Symphony Orchestra. This group performed in what was now known as the Jewish Theatre and only allowed to play pieces by Jewish composers, exclusively for Jewish audiences.

On 9 July 1942, the twenty-fifth and last concert was given. For this special occasion, Albert's podium was decorated with flowers as Monnickendam's painting depicts. A brief time later, the theatre was turned into a deportation centre. Thanks to his mixed marriage, Albert survived the war.

Yule lantern

NIOD Collection, Institute for War, Holocaust, and Genocide Studies, Amsterdam

'We cannot accept that a German Christmas tree has anything to do with a crib in a manger in Bethlehem,' wrote the Nazi propagandist Friedrich Rehm in 1937. Jesus was a Jew and Hitler and his Nazi supporters did not think people should celebrate his birthday. Besides, the Christmas message of 'peace on earth' did not correspond to Hitler's plans to conquer and subjugate large parts of Europe. The Nazis felt that the Christian Christmas celebration should be more about the 'Aryan race'.

The old Germanic Yule festival was a better fit with National Socialist ideology and it became an important SS tradition. The celebration began on 21 December, the shortest day of the year, and lasted for twelve days. During the festivities, people celebrated the gradual return of daylight. It is also known as the Germanic midwinter festival.

This traditional Yule lamp was used during the nearly two-week-long Yule festival. A Yule lamp typically held a prominent place in the homes of SS officers throughout the entire year. They were made by prisoners in the concentration camps Dachau and Neuengamme.

Street sign

Jewish Museum collection

The German occupation authority seized two school buildings in Amsterdam's Euterpestraat. On one side of the street, they set up the headquarters of the Zentralstelle für jüdische Auswanderung, the 'Central office for Jewish emigration'. The name was misleading. In fact, it was not emigration that would be overseen from this building but the deportation of Jews from the Netherlands. The headquarters of the German Sicherheitsdienst and the Gestapo – the intelligence service and secret police – were set up on the opposite side of Euterpestraat.

In the latter building, resistance fighters and Jews were often interrogated and mistreated in a brutal manner. For many detainees, 'going to Euterpestraat' often meant the start of a torturous journey past prisons and camps, frequently culminating in death. It is then not surprising that the mere mention of the name instilled mortal fear.

Shortly after the liberation, the Euterpestraat street signs, reminiscent of German terror and oppression, were replaced with ones bearing a friendlier-sounding name: Gerrit van der Veenstraat. The removal of these signs was motivated by their association with a chilling reputation, while the adoption of the new name serves as a tribute to a courageous resistance fighter who was executed on 10 June 1944.

PESTRAAT

Gravesite finds

Jewish Museum collection

After the German Wehrmacht invaded the Soviet Union, mobile military units known as *Einsatzgruppen* rounded up Jewish residents of villages and towns. In the vicinity of their homes, they were shot and thrown into mass graves. The most well-known example of such an incident is the murder of 33,771 Ukrainian Jews in the Babi Yar ravine, just outside Kiev, on 29 and 30 September 1941.

When Einsatzgruppe *C* entered the Ukrainian village of Delatyn in autumn 1941, about half of the 6,000 residents were Jewish. The Nazis forced these Jewish villagers into the nearby forest, supposedly to be put to work as manual labourers. So, the victims brought mugs, bottles and utensils with them when they were taken from their homes. But there was no work to be done; they were shot dead in the forest.

In 2015, municipal workers placed a fence around the monument at the Delatyn mass grave. While working by the memorial, they came across personal items belonging to the victims of this 1941 mass murder. Among the objects unearthed from the ground were an earring and a brooch, and several mugs and glass bottles.

Summons

Jewish Museum collection

On 20 January 1942, a meeting was held in a villa on Berlin's Lake Wannsee to discuss the fate of Europe's Jewish population. The Nazi leadership decided to murder all the Jews or use them as forced labour, ultimately leading to their deaths. The logistics of these plans were discussed at that meeting. Adolf Eichmann presented a list indicating the numbers of Jewish residents in each European country.

On 26 June 1942, the co-chairs of the Jewish Council were informed that there were plans for the 'employment of Dutch Jews'. The first 4,000 young people to be called up were notified of this on Sunday 5 July. They were expected at Amsterdam's main train station late on the evening of 14 July. The summons would serve as their travel permit. It also specified what they were allowed to bring with them. Those receiving these notices would therefore believe they were being sent to a labour camp. In reality, they were going to Auschwitz concentration and extermination camp.

Of the 4,000 individuals summoned, fewer than 1,000 turned up. For subsequent deportations, the story was the same. So, it was quickly decided to remove Jews – now entire families – from their homes. To await their deportation, a central assembly point was established in the Hollandsche Schouwburg.

Zentralstelle für jüdische
Auswanderung Amsterdam

Adama v. Scheltemaplein 1
Telefoon 97001

1

№ 19473

OPROEPING!

Aan Elisabeth Cohen
Leuvenschestr 27

Scheveningen

L 47 **No.** 13

U moet zich voor eventueele deelname aan een, onder politietoezichtstaande, werkverruiming in Duitschland voor persoonsonderzoek en geneeskundige keuring naar het doorgangskamp Westerbork, station Hooghalen, begeven.

Daartoe moet U op 19 AUG. 1942 om 1.00 uur

op de verzamelplaats DEN HAAG STAATSSPOOR — ZIE BIJLAGE — aanwezig zijn

Als bagage mag medegenomen worden:

1 koffer of rugzak
1 paar werklaarzen
2 paar sokken
2 onderbroeken
2 hemden
1 werkpak
2 wollen dekens
2 stel beddengoed (overtrek met laken)
1 eetnap
1 drinkbeker
1 lepel en
1 pullover
handdoek en toiletartikelen

en eveneens marschproviand voor 3 dagen en de voor die tijd geldige distributiekaarten.

De mee te nemen bagage moet in gedeelten gepakt worden.

a. **Noodzakelijke reisbehoeften**
daartoe behooren: 2 dekens, 1 stel beddegoed, levensmiddelen voor 3 dagen, toiletgerei, etensbord, eetbestek, drinkbeker,

b. **Groote bagage**
De onder b. vermelde bagage moet worden gepakt in een stevige koffer of rugzak, welke op duidelijke wijze voorzien moet zijn van **naam, voornamen, geboortedatum en het woord „Holland".**
Gezinsbagage is niet toegestaan.
Het voorgaande moet nauwkeurig in acht genomen worden, daar de groote bagage in de plaats van vertrek afzonderlijk ingeladen wordt.
De verschillende bewijs- en persoonspapieren mogen **niet bij de bagage verpakt worden,** doch moeten, voor onmiddellijk vertoon gereed, medegedragen worden.
De woning moet ordelijk achtergelaten en afgesloten worden, de huissleutels moeten worden medegenomen.
Niet medegenomen mogen worden: levend huisraad.

K 372

Portrait of Jan Klein by Bob Denneboom

Jewish Museum collection

Going into hiding involved significant risks, for the individuals in hiding as well as those sheltering them. In the event of betrayal or discovery, the person in hiding would face deportation, and their helper would often be severely punished. Many helpers acted out of a sense of justice, their religious beliefs, or a sense of duty. However, there were also those who did it for financial gain or took advantage of the vulnerability of those in hiding.

The Hague gymnastics teacher Jan Kasper Klein acted out of friendship and solidarity. Together with his mother and a Jewish friend in the resistance, he sheltered seventeen people. Among them was the Jewish artist Bob Denneboom and his family. Bob drew this portrait of his helper.

In February 1944, things went completely wrong. Both the people in hiding and the helpers were betrayed and arrested. Jan was first sent to Camp Vught and spent the rest of the war in concentration camp Dachau. Only four of the seventeen people in hiding survived. Because he was elsewhere at the moment of the raid, Bob was one of them. His parents, sister and brother-in-law, who were in hiding with him at the same address, were never seen again.

Gramophone record

Meertens Institute collection, Glass plate collection Phonetics, University of Amsterdam

Many Jews tried to escape deportation by legal means. For example, by obtaining the nationality of a neutral country, a baptism certificate, or a declaration of indispensability. Couples in mixed marriages were exempt from deportation, for as long as this lasted. A large number of Jews tried to prove they were of non-Jewish descent.

With the Aktie Portugesia, scientists tried to cast doubt on the ancestry of the Netherland's Portuguese Jews. This long-established Sephardic-Jewish community in the country had originally fled the Inquisition in the Iberian Peninsula at the end of the fifteenth century. Voice recordings and portrait photographs were supposed to demonstrate that Portuguese Jews differed in terms of voice, language use and appearance and therefore did not qualify as Jewish. Yehuda (Juda) Palache, the president of the Portuguese-Israelite Community in Amsterdam, was one of these Jews whose photo was taken. His voice was also recorded on this vinyl record.

The attempt to rescue the Portuguese Jews was unsuccessful. Their exemptions from deportation were revoked on 1 February 1944. Also, Juda Palache and his wife Sophia suffered the same fate. Via Theresienstadt, they ultimately ended up in Auschwitz. They were murdered there on 18 October 1944, immediately after arriving.

31 Mei '43
IIIa
Verst. 5
VT2-3 b
Fon-gr
86

St Nicholas cloak

Jewish Museum collection

Because of her marriage to the non-Jewish Flip Heil, Lien Barend had a certain level of protection from being deported. Flip helped his Jewish in-laws go into hiding and was active in the resistance. Among other things, he delivered illegal documents to people being hidden in Amsterdam. In the autumn, his resistance work was always much easier.

Through the Parool group – named for the underground newspaper they distributed – Flip got to know Mies Neeter. Due to having a non-Jewish father and not reporting her two Jewish grandparents, her marriage to the Jewish Emanuel was classified as a mixed marriage. As a result, they were exempt from deportation. They celebrated *Sinterklaas* evening every year with Flip and Lien, although Flip did not use his St Nicholas costume solely on 5 December.

In fact, the robe and mitre contained secret compartments. Because the costume also served as an excellent disguise for carrying illegal documents, to the surprise and delight of many Amsterdam children, St Nicholas arrived early in the autumn. In this way, the costume was put to optimal use. The Heil and Neeter families continued to use the St Nicholas outfit for many years after the war, although this was then limited to the holiday period.

Suitcase installation

Jewish Museum collection

In the call-up notice for so-called *tewerkstelling*, 'employment', recipients could clearly read what they needed to bring with them: a suitcase or rucksack, work boots, socks, underwear, shirts and work clothes, bedding, a bowl, spoon and a cup, a towel and toiletries. At least this way, everybody would believe they were actually going to a labour camp.

Shortly after the start of the deportations in early July 1942, a number of companies in Amsterdam saw the commercial advantage in these summonses. On 24 July, Het Joodsche Weekblad – a Jewish weekly bulletin – carried an advertisement for having rucksacks and bread sacks made by the PAZO leather goods factory, including the line: 'Priority for urgent cases'.

From the moment Jews in the Netherlands were taken from their homes for deportation, most Jewish families always had suitcases or rucksacks packed for an eventual departure. For a variety of reasons, going into hiding or fleeing was not a viable option for most of them. They anxiously awaited their fate. Nobody knew when it would be their turn to leave home, usually to never return.

Furniture Möbelaktion

Collection Museumsdorf Cloppenburg - Niedersächsisches Freilichtmuseum

With the beginning of deportations in July 1942, the German authorities also initiated their so-called furniture drive *M-Aktion*. The objective of this was the confiscation of Jewish household belongings from throughout Western Europe. The furniture was either sold at public auction or donated to German families with war-related damages to their homes.

In Amsterdam, it was the Puls moving company that cleared out the houses of Jews. After the residents had been deported or gone into hiding, their dwelling was sealed so nobody could smuggle out any household effects. Once the removal firm had visited the home in question, it was said to have been 'pulsed' – according to the newly-created verb to describe what had actually happened.

Altogether, in France, Belgium and the Netherlands, over seventy thousand homes of Jews were plundered in a similar way. Approximately one million cubic metres of household goods were shipped to Germany. The furniture stolen in the Netherlands mainly went to Northern and Western Germany, including these bedside cabinets that ended up in German hands via the Dutch M-Aktion.

Torah fragment

Jewish Museum collection

In 1944, the Polish-Jewish lawyer Raphael Lemkin, who fled to America as a refugee in 1941, coined the term 'genocide'. He described it as the systematic and planned annihilation of a population group. Besides physically eliminating the members of the victimized group, destroying the culture of the people affected is a crucial component of genocide.

All across occupied Europe, the Nazis not only eradicated the presence of Jews but also sought to eliminate their history, culture and heritage. In the Netherlands, the Van Gelder paper processing plant in the village of Velsen-Noord was among the facilities used for this end. Books on Jewish history, Jewish culture and Jewish prayer books were taken there to be destroyed. In some instances, even entire libraries of Jews who had been deported were brought to this factory.

Torah scrolls could not be shredded as easily as regular books because they are not written on paper but on parchment. This surviving fragment is a text from Acharei Mot, a parashah (portion) of the Torah. This portion is read during the morning service on the Jewish holiday of Yom Kippur, the Day of Atonement.

Film footage

Commander Gemmeker of Westerbork gave the German-Jewish photographer Rudolf Breslauer the task of documenting life in the transit camp. He shot film footage of people working inside and outside the camp as well as cabaret performances, daily activities, football matches and children painting handcrafted animal figures in the wood shop.

On 19 May 1944, Rudolf filmed a deportation train about to leave the camp. The part destined for Auschwitz was comprised of freight wagons. The prisoners in the remaining cars were headed to Bergen-Belsen. The footage shows prisoners walking towards the train, the Sinti girl Settela Steinbach gazing out of one of the cars before the doors are shut and the train finally pulling away. These are the only known moving images of a deportation train.

Rudolf never got the chance to complete the film. He and his family were deported to Theresienstadt on 4 September 1944 and from there, a while later, to Auschwitz. His wife Bella and sons Mischa and Stefan were gassed immediately upon arrival. Rudolf himself perished somewhere in Central Europe in February 1945. Only his daughter Ursula survived the Shoah.

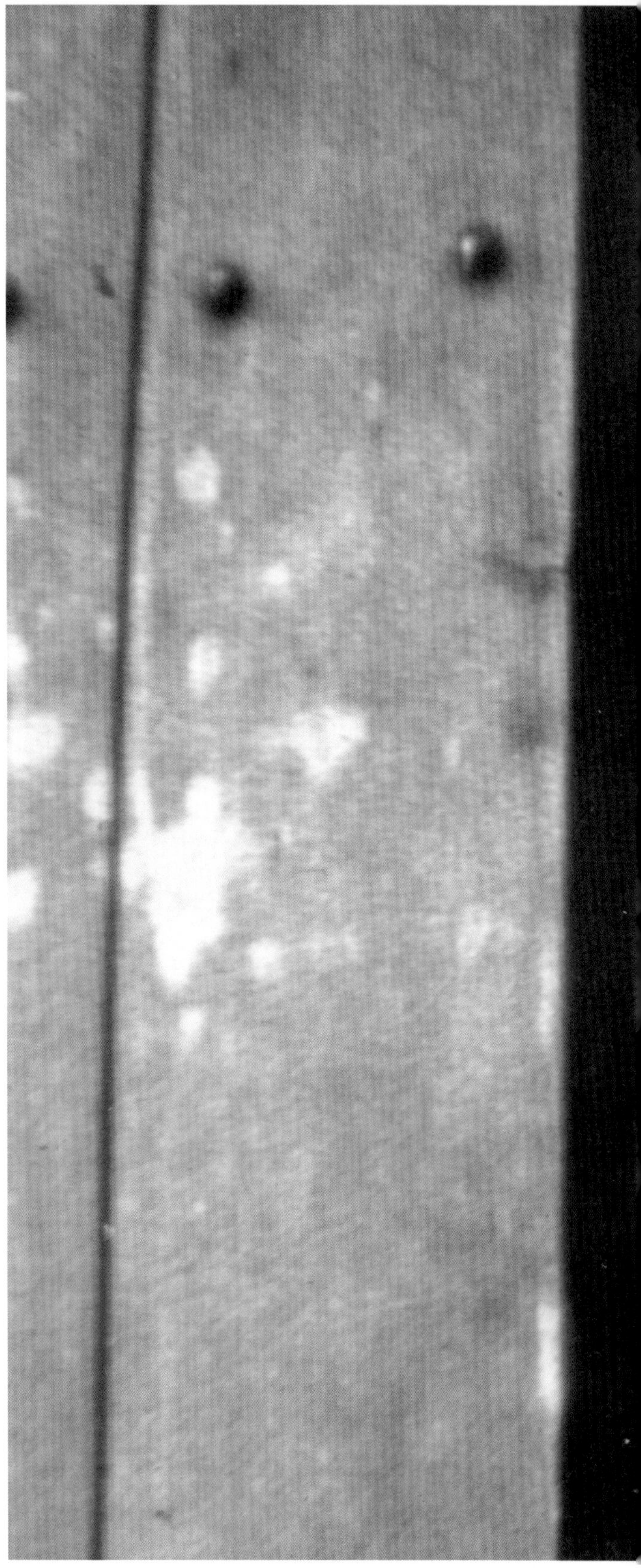

Landscape drawing

Jewish Museum collection

In the summer of 1943, the German occupier began implementing measures targeting Roma and Sinti. From 10 June, they were no longer permitted to move their caravans to the three coastal provinces of the Netherlands, Friesland or Groningen. From 22 June, Roma and Sinti were forced to live in assembly camps and by 1 July they were entirely forbidden from moving their caravans. Six months later, the Jewish prisoner Joseph Henri Gosschalk made this drawing of caravans just outside Westerbork transit camp.

On 16 May 1944, 578 Roma and Sinti were rounded up from places throughout the Netherlands and taken to Westerbork. Once there, it was discovered that 54 of them held passports from a neutral or Allied country. It was determined that 279 of the Roma and Sinti actually did not fall under the classification 'Gypsy'. Three days after their arrival in Westerbork, the remaining 245 were deported to Auschwitz-Birkenau.

Roma and Sinti were detained together at Birkenau in what the Nazis designated as the *Zigeuner-familienlager*, 'Gypsy' family camp. On 2 August 1942, this section of Birkenau was cleared of prisoners. Almost all of them were murdered in the gas chambers. Only 31 who were Dutch survived the *Porajmos*, as the persecution and murder of Roma and Sinti is called.

Radio valves

Jewish Museum collection

In December 1942, Commander of the SS Heinrich Himmler ordered the increased use of concentration camp prisoners as forced labour to benefit the German war industry. Camp Vught, the only camp established and operated by the SS within the occupied Netherlands, was also designated for this purpose. After much hesitation, the Dutch light bulb company Philips complied with this order by establishing the so-called Philips *Kommando*. Many Jews, even those without any relevant experience, were put to work there. This provided them with a temporary exemption from deportation.

The components manufactured at Camp Vught were *kriegswichtig* – essential to the war effort. Besides parts for everyday products including razors, flashlights and paperclips, also radio valves like this one were produced there. The 'workers' regularly sabotaged the products and tried to keep output as low as possible.

A total of 3,125 people, both Jews and non-Jews, were 'employed' in the Philips Kommando, On 2 June 1944, the last of the Jewish workers were deported to Auschwitz. About 400 of them survived the war.

PHILIPS

Clothing brush

Collections of the Auschwitz - Birkenau State Museum in Oświęcim

Sixty-six deportation trains departed from the Netherlands for the concentration and extermination camp Auschwitz-Birkenau. After travelling three days and nights, often in freight wagons, the exhausted victims were met by aggression and shouting. Without being able to say goodbye to each other, men were separated from their wives and children.

This was followed by a selection. With a simple hand gesture, the elderly, the sick, mothers with young children and pregnant women were sent to the gas chambers. The remaining-newly arrived prisoners were herded into the camp. A process of complete dehumanization followed. A number was tattooed on their arm, all their hair was shaved off and they were tossed dirty, ill-fitting clothes. They were stripped of all their possessions.

All the baggage and clothing these arriving prisoners brought with them was taken to the so-called Kanada-barracks, large storage warehouses. There, prisoners already in the camp sorted and searched everything for valuables. Because they regularly found food, they were slightly better off than others. This section of the camp – its name a reference to the country of Canada – was also ironically called the 'land of plenty'. This clothing brush is an example of an object found in the suitcase of an Auschwitz victim. In some sense, a clothing brush represents civilisation. It also raises questions about the former owner's expectations of his or her tewerkstelling, 'employment', in the camp.

Scissors

Collection of the State Museum af Majdanek in Lublin, Poland

From 2 March 1943, a total of nineteen deportation trains left Westerbork for the Sobibor extermination camp in the east of occupied Poland. Sobibor, a relatively small camp in terms of area, was designed to murder large groups of Jews as efficiently as possible.

When the prisoners arrived in Sobibor after a three-day train journey, they saw houses alongside the platform with flowers in the windows and gardens surrounded by white fences. In certain instances, the prisoners were greeted by the camp commander, while other times, they were forcibly expelled from the train with shouting and violence. Men and women were separated from each other and herded naked along a narrow path towards the gas chamber complex. Before they were murdered, the women and girls were led past the barber barrack, where their hair was cut off. This pair of scissors was found with a few others near the stone foundation of the gas chambers.

Of the more than 34,000 Jews deported to Sobibor from the Netherlands, only 18 of them survived the war. The extermination camp remained operational until 14 October 1943. After an uprising of forced labourers that day, the camp was permanently closed and torn down.

Braids

Jewish Museum collection

In 1944, nearly 4,000 Jews were deported from Westerbork to Bergen-Belsen. These were mostly prisoners with the nationality of a neutral country or with an exit certificate for Palestine. They were imprisoned in Bergen-Belsen to eventually be exchanged for German prisoners of war being held in Palestine under British Mandate.

Rozette van Dijk, along with her husband Joseph and their daughters Elisabeth and Judith, was deported to Bergen-Belsen on 11 January 1944. Due to the advancing Soviet Red Army, from the autumn of 1944 an increasing number of Jewish prisoners from other camps were forced to go to Bergen-Belsen. As a result, living conditions there rapidly deteriorated. Many prisoners contracted typhus and the place was swarming with lice. Through Rozette's work in the mortuary she had access to disinfectants, which she also used to delouse her daughters' hair. When there was no longer enough to do this, Rozette decided to cut off Elisabeth's braids. Elisabeth kept them in an apron she wore.

On 11 April 1945, four days before the liberation of the camp, the last of three trains carrying prisoners left Bergen-Belsen headed towards Theresienstadt. Only the transport never arrived there. After two weeks of aimlessly travelling through Germany, the prisoners were liberated by the Soviet Red Army near the village of Tröbitz. Among the survivors was also the Van Dijk family.

Parochet

Jewish Museum collection

Chaim Nussbaum was born in Lithuania but spent his childhood in the seaside town of Scheveningen in the Netherlands. After his marriage in 1939, he decided to return to his homeland. When Germany invaded Lithuania in 1941, he managed to flee via Russia and Japan to the Dutch East Indies – now Indonesia. Chaim became the rabbi of a Jewish community in Batavia, now Jakarta, and a community in Bandung – both cities located on the island of Java.

On 11 January 1942, the Japanese launched an attack on the Dutch East Indies culminating in occupation two months later. Both military prisoners and civilians of European descent were interned in camps. Chaim was taken prisoner in 1943.

In the Changi prisoner-of-war camp on the near-by island of Singapore – then a British colony under Japanese occupation – Chaim assumed the role of spiritual counsellor for the other Jewish and non-Jewish prisoners. A synagogue named Ohel Jacob was even established there. Fellow-prisoner Bert Besser made this *parochet*, a curtain for the synagogue's Holy Ark. Chaim was later forced to work on the construction of the Burma Railway, infamous for the toll it took on lives. He and his wife survived the war and emigrated to Canada after the liberation.

התורה
ה׳

Last Stop Auschwitz

Jewish Museum collection

Due to his work as a doctor in Westerbork's infirmary, Eddy de Wind spent a lengthy period in the transit camp. There he also met Friedel, a nurse he married in the camp. In September 1943, they were deported together to Auschwitz. Eddy was also put to work there. Friedel ended up in Block 10, where Nazi doctors conducted brutal medical experiments on female prisoners. By the time the Soviet Red Army liberated Auschwitz on 27 January 1945, 60,000 prisoners had been sent on death marches to other camps. Among them was Friedel.

Eddy managed to stay hidden in the camp. Unaware of Friedel's fate, he struggled with the question of how to keep going. He decided to write about his experiences since his arrest in 1942, including what he witnessed in Auschwitz and the horrors he personally endured there. While still at the concentration camp after the liberation, he found a notebook in a barrack and started writing: 'How far is it to those hazy blue mountains? How wide is the plain that stretches out in the radiant spring sunshine? It's a day's march for feet that are free. A single hour on horseback at full trot. For us it is further, much further, infinitely far.'

Friedel also survived the war. In 1946, Eddy's memoirs were published in the Netherlands under the title *Eindstation Auschwitz*. In 2020, his book was released in English as *Last Stop Auschwitz: My Story of Survival from within the Camp*. This unique autobiographical account has now been translated into around thirty languages.

Rubinstein Olga
Paks Ungarn
Templom-tér 1
A 27837
Prof. Großmann Zagreb
Dr. Weill
Zielina Teschen O.S.
Olga Lebowitz

Red Cross boxes

Jewish Museum collection

Auschwitz was liberated on 27 January 1945. In the ensuing months, more and more concentration camps followed including Bergen-Belsen, Dachau, Buchenwald and Mauthausen. The latter camp was liberated on 5 May 1945, the same day the Netherlands was liberated. While the Belgian and French repatriation of former prisoners quickly got underway, this was not the case in the Netherlands. Consequently, it sometimes took months before survivors of the Shoah set foot on Dutch soil again.

The Red Cross conducted investigations of all the Dutch nationals who had been deported or deployed as workers in the wartime industry in Germany, including over 107,000 Jews. It also published reports on the trains that departed from the Netherlands to the various concentration and extermination camps. Additionally, it sought to ascertain the fate of deported individuals to inform relatives or other people they had left behind. This work was conducted by the Red Cross's Department *J*.

Of the more than 107,000 Jews deported from the Netherlands, approximately 5,000 survived the different camps. The information the Red Cross collected about victims and survivors was documented on cards stored in wooden boxes such as this one.

IV
Gr-Joss

Repatriation outfit

Jewish Museum collection

Camp survivors tried to regain their human dignity and, once they returned, sought to pick of the pieces of their lives. After a chilly, bureaucratic reception in the Netherlands, feelings of alienation and displacement were prevalent. Wearing decent shoes and clean clothing was essential to feeling like a person again.

'I arrived here in prison clothes. What I'm wearing has been borrowed from acquaintances,' wrote Emile Franken, a survivor of Auschwitz, Mauthausen and Bergen-Belsen, to his former employer, the Dutch department store Vroom & Dreesmann. He hoped to be helped with the bare necessities: 'I don't own shoes, socks, undergarments, shirts, outerwear, etc., etc.'

Rebecca Bremer-Blum was deported from the Netherlands in 1944. With a close group of friends, she survived imprisonment in five camps including Auschwitz. The support that these women offered each other during gruelling death marches – the forced evacuations of Nazi camps as the Allies advanced – was crucial to their survival. Upon returning to the Netherlands, Rebecca's only possession was the clothes she wore, including this cardigan and skirt. Rebecca had made them herself from a horse blanket in Bergen-Belsen, where she was liberated. In the Netherlands, she was reunited with her husband Isidor. He had survived the Shoah by adopting a false identity and working for the resistance.

Nuremberg closing argument

Jewish Museum collection

After the liberation, the Dutch Ministry of Justice instituted special legal proceedings with the purpose of prosecuting Dutch citizens who had collaborated, served in the German Army or been members of the Dutch Nazi Party (NSB). For the most serious cases of collaboration, the death penalty was temporarily reinstated. This ultimate punishment was also imposed on many Nazi leaders.

Former Reich Commissioner of the Netherlands Arthur Seyss-Inquart was arrested in Hamburg on 8 May 1945 and prosecuted along with twenty-one others at the Nuremberg Trials. Despite this closing argument presented by his lawyer, Seyss-Inquart was found guilty of war crimes and crimes against humanity on 1 October 1946. For this he received the death penalty, which was carried out by hanging on the night of 15 to 16 October 1946.

The Nuremberg Trials were the first of their kind in history specifically established to prosecute war criminals. The tribunal had a significant impact on international criminal law by setting in motion due process for suspects of war crimes and crimes against humanity. Well into the twenty-first century, Nazi war criminals – many of them quite elderly – still faced prosecution.

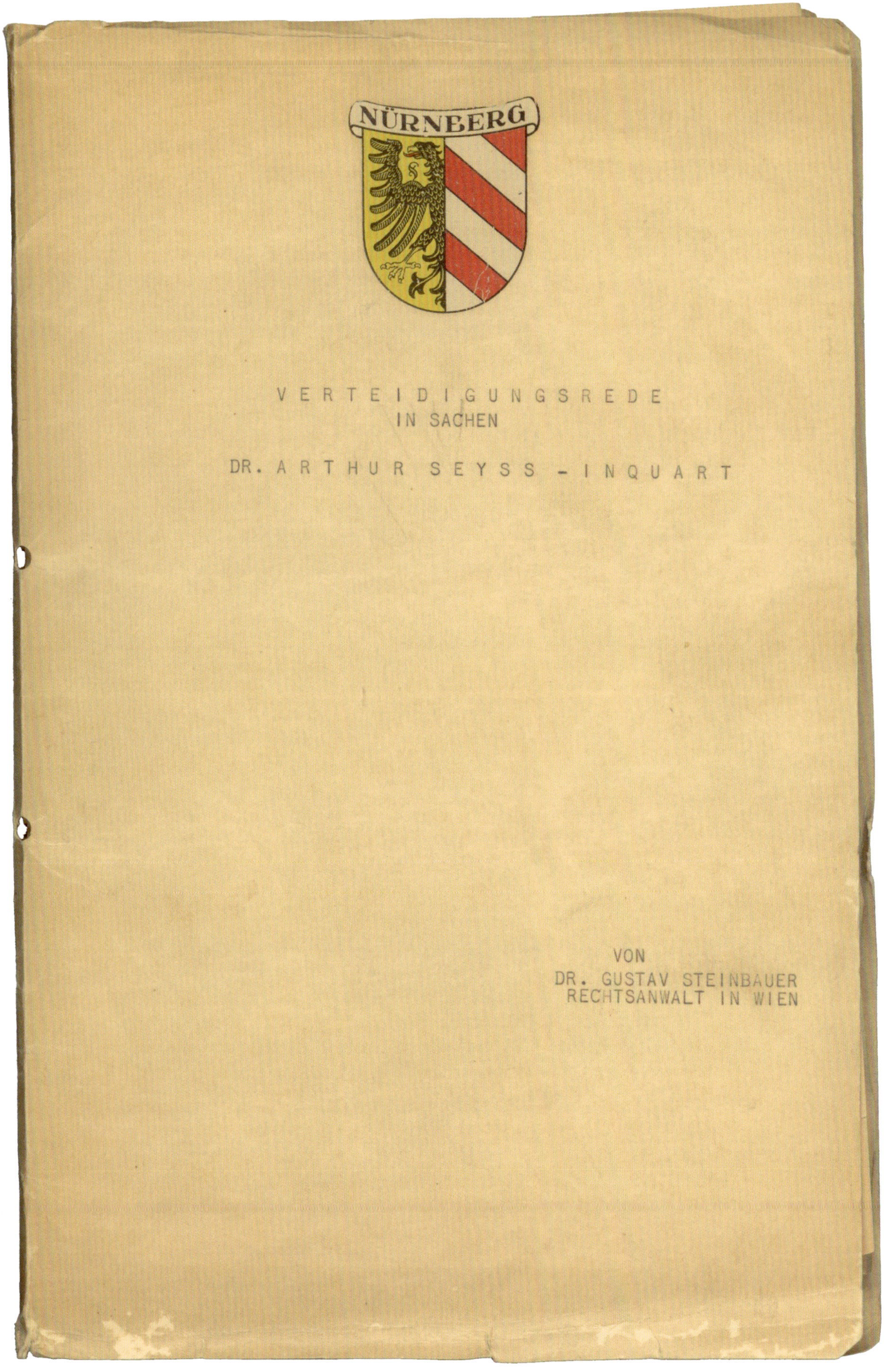
NÜRNBERG
VERTEIDIGUNGSREDE
IN SACHEN
DR. ARTHUR SEYSS-INQUART
VON
DR. GUSTAV STEINBAUER
RECHTSANWALT IN WIEN

Looted art
Henry VII and Elisabeth of York

Collection Rijksdienst voor het Cultureel Erfgoed

The NK collection includes objects brought back to the Netherlands from Germany after the Second World War with the task of returning them to their rightful owners
photo by Wendy Oakes

After the liberation, the American Army discovered depots in Germany filled with works of art. During the Nazi occupation of large parts of Europe, these had been looted from Jews and other persecuted groups, museums and collectors. Included were tens of thousands of pieces from the Netherlands that had also ended up in Germany.

Part of this artwork was eventually returned to the Netherlands and placed in the *Rijkskunst-collectie,* the National Art Collection owned by the Dutch government. Well into the 1950s, some work was returned to the original owners or their heirs, although this only involved a few hundred pieces. The recovered art that was left became part of the Netherlands Art Property Collection or NK Collection.

The NK Collection consists of art objects such as paintings, drawings and etchings, carpets, furniture and ceramics that were looted by the Nazis or purchased under duress. For instance, these sixteenth-century royal portraits, which were brought back to the Netherlands from the private collection of Nazi military leader Hermann Göring. They are believed to have originated from the art collection of a Mr Wolff from the affluent town of Wassenaar, although the evidence to support this is inconclusive.
In 2020, the Dutch government, acting on the advice of an independent committee, decided to restart the provenance research on objects from the NK Collection, hoping to trace the rightful owners – the descendants of the original owners, including those of Mr Wolfe.

Liberation (1945), Marlene Dumas

On loan from Marlene Dumas

In 1990, the Jewish Historical Museum in Amsterdam commissioned eight artists to contribute to the exhibition *Liberations*. The Amsterdam-based Marlene Dumas, who is originally from South Africa, created two pieces: *The Nuremberg Trials* – still on display at today's Jewish Museum in Amsterdam – and *Liberation (1945)*. The latter depicts a concentration camp survivor at the time of his liberation. At the height of his forehead, dozens of holes pierce the canvas. They appear as points of light, reminiscent of the infinite starry sky capable of penetrating the image's deeper darkness.

The occupation was an extremely difficult time for most people living in Netherlands. They had been oppressed, experienced fear and hunger and even lost family members. The Jews who were liberated had, despite the severity of their persecution and against all odds, survived the mass killings. Though, without family, children and community, they were denied the prospect of a future. Moreover, survivors of the Shoah often encountered a wall of misunderstanding and disinterest from the non-Jewish population. For many of the Jews who survived, the postwar period was characterised by decades of silence.

Reflecting on this portrait, Marlene Dumas explained, 'It is the face of a man who, after all the traumatic experiences he endured, is incapable of expressing joy when the liberators entered the concentration camp to free survivors.'

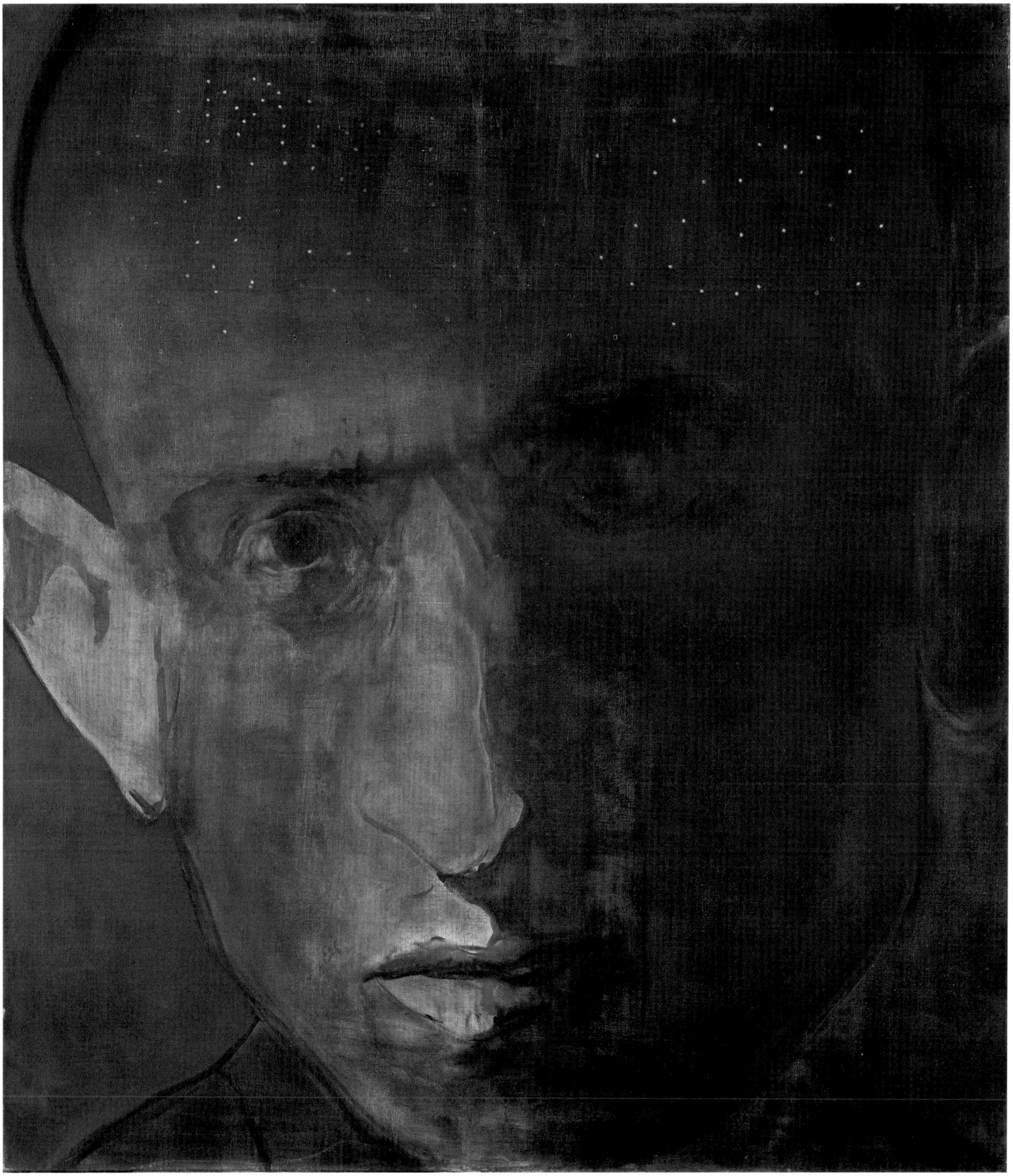

Further readings

- Bakker, A. (2005). *Dag Pap tot morgen! Joodse kinderen gered uit de crèche*. Amsterdam.
- Boom, B. van der (2022). *De politiek van het kleinste kwaad. Een geschiedenis van de Joodse Raad voor Amsterdam 1941-1943*. Amsterdam.
- Braber, B. (1990). *Zelfs als wij zullen verliezen. Joden in verzet en illegaliteit 1940-1945*. Amsterdam.
- Broersma, K. & Rossing, G. (2021). *Kamp Westerbork gefilmd. Het verhaal over een unieke film uit 1944*. Assen.
- Browning, C. R. (1993). *Doodgewone mannen*. Amsterdam.
- Campschreur, W., & Wouthuysen, E. (2022). *Jong in de oorlog. Herinneringen aan de Plantage-Weesperbuurt Amsterdam 1940-1945*. Amsterdam
- Citroen, M. (1999). *U wordt door niemand verwacht. Nederlandse Joden na kampen en onderduik*. Utrecht.
- Davids, H. (1948). *Mijn Levenslied*. Gouda.
- Flim, B. J. (1996). *Omdat hun hart sprak*. Groningen.
- Flim, B. J. (2012). *Onder de grote klok*. Leeuwarden.
- Göbel, E., & Meulenbeld, H. (2016). *Betty. Een Joodse kinderverzorgster in verzet*. Amsterdam.
- Grewel, F. (1955). De Joden van Amsterdam, II. Demografische gegevens. *Mens en Maatschappij*, 1955.
- Haan, I. de (1997). *Na de Ondergang*. Den Haag.
- Happe, K. (2018). *Veel valse hoop. De Jodenvervolging in 1940-1945 Nederland*. Amsterdam.
- Horst, W. van der. (1993). *De grond waarop wij stonden. Geschiedenis van de Hervormde Kweekschool/ Hervormde Pedagogische Akademie Amsterdam: 1907-1984*. Amsterdam.
- Kok, R. & Somers, E. (2019). *De Jodenvervolging in foto's. Nederland 1940-1945*. Zwolle.
- Kort, M. M. G. T. de (1941). *Verhandeling over de Verordening betreffende het Joodsche grondbezit (No. 154/1941)*. Amsterdam: Holdert & Co.
- Lakerveld, C. van & Levie V. (2016). *Ze doen ons niets. Vervolging en deportatie van de joden in Nederland 1940-1945*. Amsterdam.
- Levi, P. (1991) *De verdronkenen en de geredden*. Amsterdam.
- Liempt, A. van, & Kompagnie, J. H. (2011). *Jodenjacht. De onthutsende rol van de Nederlandse politie in de Tweede Wereldoorlog*. Amsterdam.
- Lipschits, I. (2001). *De kleine sjoa. Joden in naoorlogs Nederland*. Amsterdam: Mets & Schilt.
- Maandag-Ralph, K. & Skorczewski (2020). *Sieg Maandag. Life and art in the aftermath of Bergen-Belsen*. Eindhoven.
- Moore, B. (1997). *Victims and Survivors. Nazi Persecution of the Jews in the Netherlands, 1940-45*. Londen.
- Rens, H. van & Wilms, A. (2020). *Tussenstation Cosel. Joodse mannen uit West-Europa naar dwangarbeiderskampen in Silezië, 1942-1945*. Hilversum.
- Ruppert, C. (2017). *Eindelijk 'Restitutie'. De totstandkoming van Nederlandse akkoorden over Joodse oorlogstegoeden (1997-2000)*. Amsterdam: VU University Press.
- Schellekens, M. (2011). *Walter Süskind. Hoe een zakenman honderden Joodse kinderen uit handen van de nazi's redde*. Amsterdam.
- Shaya, E., & Hemminga, F. (2020). *Wacht maar. Het veelbewogen leven van Henriëtte Pimentel*. Amsterdam.
- Vree, F. van. (2010). *Iedere dag en elk uur: de Jodenvervolging en de dynamiek van de herinnering in Nederland*. In H. Berg (Ed.), *Wie niet weg is, is gezien*. Zwolle.
- Vree, F. van, Berg, H., & Duindam, D., Eds. (2012). *De Hollandsche Schouwburg: Theater, Deportatieplaats, Plek van Herinnering*. Amsterdam.
- Vree, F. van, Berg, H., & Duindam, D., Eds. (2018). *Site of deportation, site of memory. The Amsterdam Hollandsche Schouwburg and the Holocaust*. Amsterdam.
- Veraart, W. (2005). *Ontrechting en rechtsherstel in Nederland en Frankrijk in de jaren van bezetting en wederopbouw*. Deventer: Kluwer.
- Wallet, B. (2021). "'Men vrage ons niet, te vergeten': Joodse herinneringscultuur van de Tweede Wereldoorlog in Nederland." In: *Heilige Stilte: Publieke religie en de Nederlandse Dodenherdenkingen sinds 1945*. Utrecht.
- Wallet, B. (2017). "Tussen marge en centrum: Joden in naoorlogs Nederland." In: *Geschiedenis van de Joden in Nederland*. Amsterdam.
- Zwarte-Walvisch, K. de. (2009). *Alles ging aan flarden*. Amsterdam.

The Authors

Marc van Berkel is extraordinary professor of Holocaust Education at Radboud University and senior secondary-level teacher-training course lecturer at Hogeschool van Arnhem en Nijmegen (HAN University). He is a member of the Dutch delegation to the International Holocaust Remembrance Alliance (IHRA).

Esther Göbel is a researcher, curator and interviewer, and co-author of *Betty, een Joodse kinderverzorgster in verzet* (Betty, a Jewish child-care worker resists). She has published on various topics, from the Hollandsche Schouwburg to Jewish diamond workers. Esther was involved with the National Holocaust Museum permanent presentation as a researcher and curator.

Annemiek Gringold is principal curator of the National Holocaust Museum. She studied history and has worked at the Ghetto Fighters' House and Yad Vashem, both in Israel. She has published on various subjects including the Hollandsche Schouwburg and the use of firsthand documents in exhibitions. She is a member of the Dutch delegation to the International Holocaust Remembrance Alliance (IHRA).

Gerben Post is a historical researcher and author specialising in the history of the persecution of the Jews in the Netherlands. He is presently researching the history of Dutch prisoners at Mauthausen.

Julia Sarbo is a historian and studied as a teacher. She worked on educational projects for the Anne Frank Foundation and the National 4 and 5 May Committee. She has supervised educational programmes and presentation applications at the National Holocaust Museum since 2022.

Emile Schrijver is general director of the Jewish Cultural Quarter in Amsterdam and extraordinary professor of the History of the Jewish Book at the University of Amsterdam. He is editor-in-chief of *Encyclopedia of Jewish Book Cultures*.

Astrid Sy is historian, author and presenter. She has written several children's novels, has worked for NTR and presents a Dutch TV programme *Andere Tijden*. She was involved as a researcher in furnishing the historical locations at the National Holocaust Museum and the Hollandsche Schouwburg.

Wouter Veraart is professor of Encyclopaedia of Legal Studies and Philosophy of Law at Free University of Amsterdam. He is researching the role played by law in response to major injustices in history.

Asjer Waterman works for Jewish Social Work and Bibliotheca Rosenthaliana. He has previously published on the postwar history of the Ets Haim-Livraria Montezinos library.

Credits

Publisher
Waanders Publishers, Zwolle and
the National Holocaust Museum and
the Hollandsche Schouwburg

Authors
Marc van Berkel, Esther Göbel,
Annemiek Gringold, Julia Sarbo,
Emile Schrijver, Astrid Sy,
Wouter Veraert, Asjer Waterman

Editors
Annemiek Gringold, Asjer Waterman

Project management
Asjer Waterman

Translation
Sam Herman (essays)
Lorraine T. Miller (objects)

Image Editing
Charlotte Faber-Feenstra, Niels Weitkamp

Design
studio frederik de wal

Lithography
Benno Slijkhuis, Wilco Art Books

Printing
Wilco Art Books, Amersfoort

© 2024 Waanders Uitgevers b.v., Zwolle;
the National Holocaust Museum;
the authors

This publication was produced, in part, with support from the Zabawas Foundation, Tom van Praag ז״ל, and private donors.

ZABAWAS

All rights reserved. No part of the content of the book may be reproduced or transmitted in any form or by any means, electronic or mechanical, including photography, recording or any other information storage and retrieval system, without the prior written permission of the publisher.

The publisher has made every effort to acknowledge the copyright of works illustrated in this book. Should any person, despite this, feel that an omission has been made, they are requested to inform the publisher of this fact.

Copyright on works of visual artists affiliated to a CISAC organisation has been arranged with Pictoright in Amsterdam.
© c/o Pictoright Amsterdam 2024

ISBN 978 94 6262 549 5

www.waanders.nl
www.jck.nl

MIX
Paper | Supporting responsible forestry
FSC® C004472

country. **20-08-1942**: around 600 Jewish men from the city of Groningen and the surrounding area are sent to a labour camp in the Netherlands. **20-08-1942**: a total of 59 Jewish men from the city of Leeuwarden are also sent to a labour camp in the Netherlands. Followed by another 21 men from the rest of the province of Friesland. **23-08-1942**: the Academy of Fine Arts in The Hague is used as a deportation centre for the first time. 600 Jews are deported to Westerbork. **23-08-1942**: in the city of Haarlem, a few hundred Jews are called up for deportation to Westerbork. **25-08-1942**: the German police together with Dutch officers carry out a *razzia* in Haarlem. This is a direct response to not enough Jews obeying their call-up notices. **25-08-1942**: first *razzia* against Jews in the province of Limburg. **25-08-1942**: all Jews in Utrecht aged 60 and older must relocate to Amsterdam. Though around 400 of them are immediately sent to Westerbork. **27-08-1942**: hundreds of Jews from the province of North Brabant receive a call-up notice to report the very next day. Via a central assembly point in Den Bosch, they are sent to Westerbork. Most of them are deported to Auschwitz on 31 August. **29-08-1942**: near the town of Cosel in occupied Poland, around 170 Jewish men are taken from a deportation train to work as forced labour. Ultimately, 3,540 men are selected there for this same purpose from 18 deportation trains that leave Westerbork transit camp. The remaining deportees aboard these trains end up in Auschwitz. **01-09-1942**: in Amsterdam, a municipal collection service for used materials and different waste products is set up. Jews may no longer work in this sector and must hand in their buyers' permits. **01-09-1942**: Commandant Deppner of Westerbork is succeeded by Hugo Dischner. **02-09-1942**: Amsterdam police officers are ordered to remove Jews from their homes at night. Entire families are now taken. The *Zentralstelle* provides lists based on the 1941 municipal registration. **10-09-1942**: the *Politiebataljon Amsterdam* is deployed to remove Jews from their homes. In the month of September, 400 Jews are arrested during nightly raids carried out five times per week. **11-09-1942**: in The Hague, Jews are no longer permitted to sit on public benches. Violators of this ordinance are arrested and deported. **12-09-1942**: Jews in mixed marriages must now register. They are eligible for exemption from deportation. One condition is that their children are not considered Jewish. Submitting the request costs two Dutch guilders. **15-09-1942**: Jewish students are permanently banned from pursuing university education. Jews are also no longer allowed to sit for exams. **16-09-1942**: employees of the Jewish Council receive a temporary exemption from deportation. An official stamp in their identity cards now serves as proof. **18-09-1942**: Jews who go into hiding or otherwise try to escape 'employment' will be severely punished. **22-09-1942**: the Commandant of Westerbork is ordered to prepare the camp for a large arrival of prisoners. **22-09-1942**: Dutch newspapers report that four non-Jewish Dutch individuals were sent to a concentration camp for helping Jews. **23-09-1942**: the vacant housing of deported Jews in Amsterdam's Transvaal neighbourhood is made available to Jews relocating from other parts of the city. Jews from outside Amsterdam also end up in this working-class neighbourhood through forced relocation. Only the *Gemeentelijke Woningdienst*, municipal housing service, is authorised to relet the former homes of Jews. **24-09-1942**: Rauter reports to Berlin that the Jews in Dutch labour camps will be transferred to Westerbork in early October. Their family members will be reunited with them. **30-09-1942**: Hitler delivers a speech in Berlin stating that he will wipe out European Jewry. **02 and 03-10-1942**: a total of 5,242 Jewish men in Dutch labour camps are transferred to Westerbork. Their family members are removed from their homes and also taken to Westerbork. A total of 12,296 people arrive at the transit camp. **02 and 03-10-1942**: a total of 234 Jews from the city of Assen are rounded up and taken to Westerbork. **03-10-1942**: in Amsterdam, the daily round-up of Jews is mainly carried out by the *Politiebataljon Amsterdam*. Other city police officers are no longer deployed for this task. **08-10-1942**: anyone helping Jews go into hiding or involved in forging identity cards will be punished. They face imprisonment in Camp Amersfoort for at least six months. **12-10-1942**: Commandant Dischner of Westerbork is replaced by Albert Konrad Gemmeker. **15-10-1942**: Jews from Amsterdam's Rivierenbuurt in the south of the city must move to the Transvaalbuurt, a neighbourhood in the east of the city. **16-10-1942**: Seyss-Inquart decides that Jews converted to Protestantism and Jews in mixed marriages with children are exempt from deportation. **16-10-1942**: 150 Dutch men from the Police Training Battalion, stationed in the village of Schalkhaar, are deployed to assist the *Politiebataljon Amsterdam* with the removal of Jews from their homes. These men have been trained in accordance with National Socialist ideology. **19-10-1942**: Jews are forbidden to move to Amsterdam from anywhere else in North Holland. As of 28 October, it will also be forbidden to move within Amsterdam without a permit. This ban does not apply to Jews who are ordered by the occupier to relocate to designated Amsterdam neighbourhoods. **20-10-1942**: Dutch Jews living in the unoccupied part of France (Free Zone) are granted permission by the Dutch government-in-exile to leave for the Dutch colony of Suriname on the northern coast of South America. The German authorities put an end to this on 11 November. **30-10-1942**: Dutch police officers are required to carry out the arrest, transport and any preliminary hearings of Jews, hostages and others. **02-11-1942**: the railway line between Hooghalen Station and Westerbork is completed. Now Jews can be directly deported from the transit camp 'to the East'. **11-11-1942**: a *razzia* is carried out in the Hollandia Kattenburg raincoat factory in the north of Amsterdam. Due to suspected connections with the Dutch resistance, the 367 Jewish employees are arrested. Their family members are removed from their homes. Everyone is taken to Westerbork. **11-11-1942**: first deportation of Jews from the city of Bergen op Zoom to Westerbork transit camp. **12-11-1942**: another 95 Jews are deported from the city of Leeuwarden to Westerbork. **17-11-1942**: in the city of Arnhem, 200 Jews are rounded up overnight and deported to Westerbork. **17-11-1942**: in the city of Nijmegen, 200 Jews are rounded up overnight and deported to Westerbork. **24-11-1942**: the Dutch government in London announces that it is forbidden to use foreign currency to purchase the freedom of Jews. **27-11-1942**: a *razzia* takes place in Amsterdam targeting clothing workshops previously owned by Jews. **31-12-1942**: Jewish patients and Jews in hiding at the Rosenburg psychiatric clinic in The Hague are rounded up. Most of them are deported via Westerbork to Auschwitz two weeks later. **31-12-1942**: as many as 38,578 Jews are deported from the Netherlands in 1942. **1943** **01-01-1943**: the banking institute Lippmann, Rosenthal & Co., which has looted Jewish assets since being seized by the German occupier, stops providing income support to Jewish households. From now on, the Jewish Council assumes financial responsibility for these families. **05-01-1943**: acts of sabotage and the disruption of public order and security become punishable by death. **06-01-1943**: deportation of 80 Jewish patients from Zuidwal Hospital in The Hague to Westerbork. **08-01-1943**: departments of Amsterdam's Jewish Council may no longer contact the *Hollandsche Schouwburg* by telephone. The exception is the Expositur, the council's liaison office with the occupation authorities. **08-01-1943**: a list of people provisionally exempted from deportation created by a Jewish man named Frederich Weinreb is declared invalid. On this fictitious emigration list are the names of Jews who believed they had purchased an exemption from Weinreb after paying him a large sum of money. **13-01-1943**: the recently built Vught concentration camp supervised by the SS goes into operation. **14-01-1943**: from now on, all abandoned infants and children will be considered Jewish. **16-01-1943**: the first 500 Jewish detainees from the *Hollandsche Schouwburg* arrive at Camp Vught expecting to be put to work there. But they will later still be deported from the Netherlands. **18-01-1943**: Jewish employees of the *Gemeentelijke Werk-inrichting voor Blinden*, a municipal institute in Amsterdam providing work for the blind, are rounded up and deported. **20-01-1943**: Jews are also now removed from their homes in broad daylight. These are mainly Jews previously exempt from deportation due to poor health. **21-01-1943**: around 1,200 Jewish patients of the Jewish psychiatric clinic *Het Apeldoornsche Bosch* are rounded up during the night. Part of the staff is sent to Westerbork. The remaining employees and residents are deported directly to Auschwitz. There they are murdered immediately upon arrival. **29-01-1943**: it is determined in Berlin that Roma and Sinti must also be deported to Auschwitz. This measure is scheduled to go into effect in the Netherlands on 29 March 1943 but is only first implemented in 1944. **30-01-1943**: studying Hebrew as a classical language may no longer be included in the teaching curriculums of gymnasiums. **04-02-1943**: in retaliation for a shooting incident, 207 Jews from the provinces of Groningen and Friesland who have exemptions from deportation are still rounded up and deported to Westerbork. Their exemptions are invalidated. **05-02-1943**: Jews are no longer allowed to have direct contact with the occupation authorities. All contact must now go via the Jewish Council. **10-02-1943**: Jewish orphanages in Amsterdam are emptied. A total of 250 children and their caregivers are deported to Westerbork. **12-02-1943**: Jews may no longer live in the cities of Haarlem, Heemstede, Bloemendaal, Aerdenhout and Voorschoten and are ordered to relocate to Amsterdam. **14-02-1943**: the *Politiebataljon Amsterdam* no longer removes Jews from their homes. This is now done by the *Vrijwillige Hulppolitie*, comprised of volunteers from the NSB and Dutch SS. **23-02-1943**: the Dutch government-in-exile considers exchanging Dutch Jews for German prisoners of war. However, the proposal is rejected because the London Cabinet is not convinced Jews should be given 'preferential treatment'. **02-03-1943**: a reward of 7.50 in Dutch guilders is offered for tracking down and turning in Jews in hiding. Those who violate other anti-Jewish regulations are also betrayed. This bounty per head, called *kopgeld*, comes from confiscated Jewish assets. **02-03-1943**: during the night, the first of 19 deportation trains to Sobibor extermination camp leaves Westerbork. Aboard are 1,105 Jewish men, women and children. **13-03-1943**: newly-built large gas chambers with crematoriums at Auschwitz-Birkenau are put into operation. **17-03-1943**: the last Jews from the city of Leiden are deported to Westerbork. Included among them are 50 orphans. **19-03-1943**: Jews with a special authorization to use trams must always show the driver their permit. **29-03-1943**: as of 10 April, Jews are no longer allowed to be anywhere in the provinces of Friesland, Groningen, Drenthe, Overijssel, Gelderland, Limburg, North Brabant and Zeeland. They must report to Camp Vught. **01-04-1943**: Dutch civil servants married to Jews are dismissed. Exceptions are granted if a marriage has previously ended due to death or divorce. **01-04-1943**: Jews may no longer be cared for by non-Jewish nurses. **05-04-1943**: streets and squares in The Hague that are named after Jews are renamed. **13-04-1943**: as of 23 April, Jews may no longer live in the provinces of Utrecht, South Holland and North Holland – with the exception of Amsterdam. They are ordered to report to Camp Vught. **19-04-1943**: mortgages given to Jews may be cancelled. Later, the *Landelijke Hypotheekbank*, the national mortgage bank, is ordered to take over and foreclose on these homeowner loans. Revenues from the sale of Jewish property are transferred to the LiRo. **21-04-1943**: the first deportation train from the Netherlands to Theresienstadt concentration camp, in what was then Czechoslovakia, departs with 296 Jews from the *Hollandsche Schouwburg* in Amsterdam aboard. **22-04-1943**: hundreds of Jews are deported to Camp Vught from Utrecht, North and South Holland. Only the caretakers of Jewish cemeteries in these provinces are excluded from deportation. **23-04-1943**: only in Amsterdam are Jews allowed to stay in their own homes. Outside of Amsterdam, as an exception, also Jews in mixed marriages may stay in their houses. **29-04-1943**: guidelines are proposed by Rauter about the further 'de-Jewification' of the Netherlands, preparations for the deportation of the last Jews from Amsterdam, the relocation of children from mixed marriages, and the deportation of the Barneveld group – prominent Jews granted special exemptions – to Theresienstadt. **05-05-1943**: secret new instructions entitled the 'final solution to the Jewish problem in the Netherlands' are issued. Exemptions from deportation will be declared invalid. The last Jews will be deported from Amsterdam to Camp Vught, which will serve as a transit camp. **05-05-1943**: Jews in mixed marriages must have themselves sterilised or present official proof of infertility. Afterwards, they may remove the yellow star from their clothing. **06-05-1943**: Jewish suppliers of goods and wholesalers lose their exemptions from deportation and are arrested. **14-05-1943**: an announcement that as of 21 May, Jews will be forbidden from being anywhere in Amsterdam. Jews with deportation exemptions are excluded from this measure. **14-05-1943**: at Westerbork, more than 100 Jews in mixed marriages are forced to choose between

sterilisation or deportation – 51 of them choose 'voluntary' sterilisation. **20-05-1943**: repeat announcement that a
for 'employment in Germany'. Turnout is low. **21-05-1943**: the Jewish Council is instructed to select 7,000 Jews who
the council agrees to comply. **25-05-1943**: of the 7,000 Jews summoned to report for 'employment', 546 turn up. T
Amsterdam's Jewish quarter with no regard for exemptions: 3,435 Jewish men, women and children are rounded
parents and guardians aboard. During these 'transports' of children, 3,017 Jews are deported via Westerbork to So
their caravans to three of the coastal provinces of the Netherlands and large parts of Friesland and Groningen. **11-**
London, the Swedish government requests that Jewish children from the Netherlands be allowed to go to Palest
large *razzias* take place in the Transvaal neighbourhood in the east of Amsterdam, and in the south of Amsterdam
to relocate to assembly camps. A total of 27of these camps are set up. This gathering of Roma and Sinti is the pr
These include sterilisation and relocation. They are also exempted from wearing the yellow star. **29-06-1943**: the
officially lose their right to civil justice. From now on they are subject to police justice. **01-07-1943**: Roma and Sint
members of the Dutch resistance are executed. All of them took part in the bombing of Amsterdam's population
forbidden from including letters with packages sent to camps such as Westerbork and Vught. **23-07-1943**: in Amst
among them are 70 children and 36 staff members from the Crèche, the deportation centre's nursery, directly acr
provinces of Groningen, Friesland, Drenthe, Gelderland and Overijssel for men over age 16 who are officially liste
community's hospital in Amsterdam are deported to Westerbork. The last Jewish hospital is now closed. **26-08-**
from Auschwitz leaves for the new Camp Warsaw. Among them are hundreds of Dutch Jews. They are put to wor
uprising of Jewish fighters that began on 19 April 1943 and lasted five weeks. **13-09-1943**: Jews in mixed marriag
Obrechtplein in Amsterdam is commandeered and put to use as the headquarters of the German army's nursin
market temporarily set up for Jewish shoppers on the playground in Gaaspstraat are permanently shut down. **17-**
250 residents and staff are deported to Westerbork. There are now no longer any Jewish healthcare facilities in the
The 2,000 Jews deported to Westerbork include the leaders of the Jewish Council. The Netherlands is officially 'fr
huis, a Jewish boys' orphanage in Amsterdam, is commandeered by the German army. **05-10-1943**: new guidelin
obligation to report, bans on certain occupations and a red capital J being stamped on their identity cards. **07-10-1**
Jews in the homes of Amsterdam Jews – is shut down. **14-10-1943**: after the prisoner revolt at Sobibor, the camp
took place there. **19-11-1943**: the last Jews arrested in hiding are deported from the *Hollandsche Schouwburg* to We
notices for a labour camp in the Netherlands. **1944** **01-01-1944**: as of this date, prisoners in Japanese internmen
mixed marriages receive health checks and are approved for forced labour in the *Amsterdam Bos*, a woodland area
adults and children are aboard the train. **18-01-1944**: a total of 900 Jewish men in mixed marriages are deployed
status reports on the deportations of the Jews and tracking down Jews in hiding and their helpers. **01-02-1944**: an
about their Jewish ancestry. These Jews are deported to Westerbork from the cities of Amsterdam, Rotterdam, Le
Auschwitz. The train leaves with a total of 1,015 people. **20-02-1944**: it is determined by the German authorities tha
ancestry. **26-02-1944**: preparations to deport prisoners whose Jewish ancestry is ambiguous from Westerbork to
as forced labour. **28-02-1944**: Seyss-Inquart puts forward proposals on the treatment of Jews married to non-Jews
1944: in a letter to the Nazi-authority in Berlin, Rauter discusses his position on Jews married to non-Jews and th
still under examination. They will be deported to Bergen-Belsen. **31-03-1944**: Jews in mixed marriages are rounde
wagons packed with Jewish deportees from the Belgian transit camp in Mechelen and wagons from Westerbor
Auschwitz. **29-04-1944**: the head of the Japanese military administration in the Dutch East Indies gives a fierce
requires presenting your identity card to the authorities. This makes it much more difficult for people in hiding, b
Roma and Sinti must be arrested and deported. A day later, local police departments of several major cities recei
576 of them are taken to Westerbork. More than half of them are released two days later. **19-05-1944**: from Weste
Auschwitz-Birkenau. **03-06-1944**: the last deportation of Jewish prisoners from Camp Vught to Auschwitz. Aboard
allegations surface about the use of false documents, the non-Jewish identity of 3,709 people must be reconfirm
Jews in mixed marriages and Jews in hiding are still in the country. Those still in hiding must be tracked down and a
labour. The rest of the prisoners, over 4,000 people, are gassed. Among them are also Roma and Sinti from the Ne